Mastering

A Compr

Mastering C# - A Comprehensive Guide

Ocirema and Américo Moreira

Published by Américo Moreira, 2023.

While every precaution has been taken in the preparation of this book, the publisher assumes no responsibility for errors or omissions, or for damages resulting from the use of the information contained herein.

MASTERING C# - A COMPREHENSIVE GUIDE

First edition. November 11, 2023.

ISBN: 979-8223692102

Written by Ocirema and Américo Moreira.

Table of Contents

1 - Introduction to C#

1.1 History of C#

C# (pronounced C sharp) is a modern, object-oriented programming language developed by Microsoft Corporation. It was created by Anders Hejlsberg and his team at Microsoft during the late 1990s as part of the .NET initiative. C# was designed to be a simple, yet powerful language that combines the best features of C++ and Java.

1.1.1 Origins of C#

The development of C# can be traced back to the early 1990s when Microsoft was working on the development of its flagship operating system, Windows. At that time, Microsoft primarily used C and C++ for system-level programming. However, these languages had their limitations, and Microsoft wanted a language that could provide better productivity and ease of use.

In 1995, Microsoft released the first version of its Java Virtual Machine (JVM) implementation, called "Microsoft Java Virtual Machine." However, due to legal disputes with Sun Microsystems, the creators of Java, Microsoft had to discontinue its JVM. This setback prompted Microsoft to develop its own programming language that could run on the .NET platform.

1.1.2 Birth of C#

The development of C# began in the late 1990s when Microsoft started working on the .NET initiative. The goal of .NET was to create a platform that would allow developers to build and deploy applications across different devices and operating systems. To achieve this, Microsoft needed a new programming language that could take full advantage of the .NET platform.

Anders Hejlsberg, a renowned Danish software engineer, was chosen to lead the development of C#. Hejlsberg had previously worked on the development of Turbo Pascal and Borland Delphi, two popular programming languages. He brought his expertise and experience to the development of C#, ensuring that the language would be both powerful and easy to use.

1.1.3 Influences on C#

C# draws inspiration from several programming languages, including C++, Java, and Delphi. The syntax of C# is similar to that of C++, making it familiar to developers who are already proficient in C or C++. C# also borrows many concepts from Java, such as garbage collection and exception handling.

One of the key influences on C# is the Component Object Model (COM), a technology developed by Microsoft for building software components. C# was designed to seamlessly integrate with COM, allowing developers to create COM components using the language.

1.1.4 Evolution of C#

C# has evolved significantly since its initial release. The first version of C#, known as C# 1.0, was released in 2002 as part of the .NET Framework 1.0. This version introduced the core features of the language, including classes, objects, inheritance, and exception handling.

Over the years, Microsoft has released several new versions of C#, each introducing new features and improvements. Some notable versions include C# 2.0, which introduced generics and anonymous methods, and C# 3.0, which introduced LINQ (Language Integrated Query) and lambda expressions.

C# 4.0 introduced dynamic typing, allowing developers to write code that can adapt to different types at runtime. C# 5.0 introduced async/await, making it easier to write asynchronous code. C# 6.0 introduced several new features, including null-conditional operators and string interpolation.

The most recent version of C# is C# 9.0, which was released in 2020. This version introduced several new features, including records, pattern matching enhancements, and improved support for nullable reference types.

1.1.5 Popularity and Adoption

C# has gained significant popularity and adoption since its release. It is widely used for developing a variety of applications, including desktop applications, web applications, mobile apps, and games. C# is the primary language used for developing applications on the Microsoft .NET platform.

C# is known for its simplicity, readability, and robustness. It provides a rich set of features that make it easy to write clean and maintainable code. The language has a large and active community of developers who contribute to its growth and development.

C# is also widely used in the enterprise software development industry. Many large organizations and companies rely on C# for building mission-critical applications. The language's integration with the .NET platform and its support for industry-standard technologies make it a popular choice for enterprise development.

In conclusion, C# is a powerful and versatile programming language that has evolved over the years to become one of the most popular languages in the software development industry. Its rich set of features, simplicity, and strong integration with the .NET platform have contributed to its widespread adoption. Understanding the history of C# provides a solid foundation for mastering the language and leveraging its capabilities to build robust and scalable applications.

1.2 Features of C#

C# (pronounced as "C sharp") is a powerful and versatile programming language developed by Microsoft. It was first introduced in the early 2000s as part of the .NET framework and has since become one of the most popular programming languages in the world. C# is widely used for developing a wide range of applications, including desktop, web, mobile, and gaming applications.

C# is known for its rich set of features that make it a preferred choice for many developers. In this section, we will explore some of the key features of C# that make it a powerful and flexible programming language.

1.2.1 Object-Oriented Programming

C# is a fully object-oriented programming language, which means that it supports the principles of encapsulation, inheritance, and polymorphism. Object-oriented programming (OOP) allows developers to organize their code into reusable objects, making it easier to manage and maintain large-scale applications. With C#, you can define classes, create objects from those classes, and interact with them using methods and properties.

1.2.2 Strong Typing

C# is a strongly typed language, which means that every variable and expression must have a specific type. This helps catch errors at compile-time and ensures that the code is more robust and less prone to runtime errors. Strong typing also enables the compiler to perform type checking and provide better code completion and IntelliSense support in integrated development environments (IDEs).

1.2.3 Garbage Collection

C# includes automatic memory management through a process called garbage collection. Garbage collection relieves developers from manually allocating and deallocating memory, reducing the risk of memory leaks and other memory-related issues. The garbage collector automatically identifies and frees up memory that is no longer in use, improving the overall performance and reliability of C# applications.

1.2.4 Language Interoperability

C# is designed to be highly interoperable with other programming languages. It can seamlessly integrate with other .NET languages, such as Visual Basic.NET and F#, allowing developers to leverage existing code and libraries written in different languages. C# also supports interoperability with native code through platform invoke and COM interop, enabling developers to use functionality from external libraries and components.

1.2.5 Asynchronous Programming

C# provides robust support for asynchronous programming, allowing developers to write efficient and responsive applications. Asynchronous programming enables tasks to run concurrently, freeing up the main thread to perform other operations. C# includes keywords such as async and await that simplify the process of writing asynchronous code, making it easier to handle time-consuming operations without blocking the user interface.

1.2.6 Exception Handling

Exception handling is an essential aspect of writing reliable and robust code. C# provides a comprehensive exception handling mechanism that allows developers to catch and handle exceptions gracefully. With features like try-catch-finally blocks, developers can write code that handles exceptional situations and recovers from errors without crashing the application. C# also supports custom exceptions, enabling developers to define their own exception types for specific scenarios.

1.2.7 Language Integrated Query (LINQ)

LINQ is a powerful feature of C# that allows developers to query and manipulate data from different sources, such as databases, collections, and XML documents, using a unified syntax. LINQ provides a set of standard query operators that can be used to perform filtering, sorting, grouping, and aggregation operations on data. This simplifies the process of working with data and makes code more readable and maintainable.

1.2.8 Generics

Generics in C# enable developers to write reusable code that can work with different types. By using generics, developers can create classes, methods, and data structures that are parameterized by one or more types. This allows for type-safe and efficient code, as the compiler performs type checking at compile-time. Generics also promote code reuse and reduce the need for casting and boxing/unboxing operations.

1.2.9 Integrated Development Environment (IDE) Support

C# is well-supported by various integrated development environments (IDEs), such as Visual Studio, Visual Studio Code, and JetBrains Rider. These IDEs provide a rich set of tools and features that enhance productivity and make development easier. Features like code completion, debugging, refactoring, and version control integration help developers write high-quality code efficiently.

In conclusion, C# is a feature-rich programming language that offers a wide range of capabilities for developing robust and scalable applications. Its support for object-oriented programming, strong typing, garbage collection, and other advanced features make it a popular choice among developers. Whether you are a beginner or an experienced programmer, mastering C# will open up a world of possibilities for building diverse and powerful applications.

1.3 Setting up C# Development Environment

Setting up your C# development environment is the first step towards becoming a proficient C# programmer. In this section, we will guide you through the process of installing the necessary tools and configuring your environment to start writing and running C# code.

1.3.1 Installing Visual Studio

The most popular and widely used integrated development environment (IDE) for C# programming is Microsoft Visual Studio. Visual Studio provides a comprehensive set of tools and features that make it easier to write, debug, and deploy C# applications.

To install Visual Studio, follow these steps:

1. Visit the official Visual Studio website at .
2. Click on the "Download" button to download the Visual Studio installer.
3. Run the installer and follow the on-screen instructions to install Visual Studio.
4. During the installation process, you will be prompted to select the workloads and components you want to install. For C# development, make sure to select the ".NET desktop development" workload, which includes the necessary tools and libraries for C# programming.
5. Once the installation is complete, launch Visual Studio.

1.3.2 Configuring Visual Studio

After installing Visual Studio, you need to configure it to ensure that it is set up correctly for C# development. Here are some important configuration steps:

1. Select a theme: Visual Studio offers different themes to

customize the appearance of the IDE. You can choose a theme that suits your preferences by going to "Tools" > "Options" > "Environment" > "General" and selecting your desired theme from the "Color theme" dropdown menu.

2. Configure font and text size: You can adjust the font and text size in Visual Studio to improve readability. Go to "Tools" > "Options" > "Environment" > "Fonts and Colors" to customize the font and text size settings.

3. Set up code formatting preferences: Visual Studio allows you to define your code formatting preferences to ensure consistent and readable code. Go to "Tools" > "Options" > "Text Editor" > "C#" > "Code Style" to configure your code formatting preferences.

4. Install extensions: Visual Studio supports a wide range of extensions that can enhance your development experience. You can browse and install extensions from the Visual Studio Marketplace by going to "Extensions" > "Manage Extensions".

1.3.3 Creating a New C# Project

Once you have installed and configured Visual Studio, you are ready to create your first C# project. Follow these steps to create a new C# project:

1. Open Visual Studio.

2. Click on "Create a new project" on the start page, or go to "File" > "New" > "Project".

3. In the "Create a new project" window, select "Visual C#" from the left-hand menu.

4. Choose the type of project you want to create. For example, you can select "Console App (.NET Core)" to create a console application.

5. Enter a name and location for your project, and click on the "Create" button.
6. Visual Studio will create the project and open the main code file for you to start writing your C# code.

1.3.4 Running a C# Program

To run a C# program in Visual Studio, follow these steps:

1. Make sure the code file containing your C# program is open in the editor.
2. Press the "Ctrl + F5" keys or go to "Debug" > "Start Without Debugging" to run the program.
3. The output of the program will be displayed in the console window.

1.3.5 Using an Alternative Development Environment

While Visual Studio is the most popular choice for C# development, there are alternative development environments available that you can use. Some popular alternatives include:

-   Visual Studio Code: A lightweight and cross-platform code editor that supports C# development with the help of extensions.
-   JetBrains Rider: A powerful and cross-platform IDE specifically designed for .NET development, including C#.

These alternative development environments offer similar features and capabilities to Visual Studio, but with different user interfaces and workflows. You can choose the one that best suits your preferences and requirements.

In this section, we have covered the process of setting up your C# development environment, including installing Visual Studio, configuring the IDE, creating a new C# project, and running a C# program. With your environment ready, you are now equipped to dive into the world of C# programming and explore the various concepts and features covered in this book.

1.4 Your First C# Program

In this section, we will guide you through the process of writing and running your first C# program. This will give you a hands-on experience with the C# programming language and help you understand the basic structure of a C# program.

1.4.1 Setting up the Development Environment

Before we start writing our first C# program, we need to set up the development environment. To write and run C# programs, we will be using Visual Studio, a popular integrated development environment (IDE) for C#.

1. Download and install Visual Studio: Visit the official Microsoft website and download the latest version of Visual Studio. Follow the installation instructions provided by the installer.

2. Launch Visual Studio: Once the installation is complete, launch Visual Studio from your desktop or start menu.

3. Create a new project: In Visual Studio, go to "File" > "New" > "Project" to create a new project. Select "Console App (.NET Core)" as the project template and provide a name for your project.

4. Write your first C# program: Visual Studio will create a default C# program for you. You will see a file named "Program.cs" open in the editor. This is where we will write our first C# code.

1.4.2 Understanding the Structure of a C# Program

Before we dive into writing our first C# program, let's take a moment to understand the structure of a C# program. A C# program consists of one or more classes, and each class can contain methods, properties, and variables.

The default C# program created by Visual Studio contains a class named "Program" with a method named "Main". The "Main" method is the entry point of a C# program, and it is where the program execution starts.

Here is the basic structure of a C# program:

```
using System;
namespace YourNamespace
{
class Program
{
static void Main(string[] args)
{
// Your code goes here
}
}
}
```

Let's break down the different parts of this structure:

- using System;: This line is called a using directive and it allows us to use types from the System namespace without fully qualifying their names.
- namespace YourNamespace: A namespace is a way to organize related code. It helps prevent naming conflicts between different parts of a program. You can choose any name for your namespace.
- class Program: A class is a blueprint for creating objects. In this case, we have a class named "Program" which contains our main method.
- static void Main(string[] args): This is the entry point of our program. The "Main" method is static, which means it belongs to the class itself and not to any specific instance of the class.

It takes an array of strings as a parameter, which can be used to pass command-line arguments to the program.

1.4.3 Writing Your First C# Program

Now that we understand the structure of a C# program, let's write our first C# program. In this example, we will write a simple program that displays the message "Hello, World!" on the console.

Replace the existing code in the "Main" method with the following code:

```
Console.WriteLine("Hello, World!");
```

That's it! You have just written your first C# program. The Console.WriteLine statement is used to display text on the console. In this case, it will display the message "Hello, World!".

1.4.4 Running Your C# Program

To run your C# program, simply click the "Start" button in Visual Studio or press the "F5" key. Visual Studio will build your program and execute it.

You should see the output "Hello, World!" displayed in the console window. Congratulations, you have successfully run your first C# program!

1.4.5 Modifying Your C# Program

Now that you have written and run your first C# program, feel free to experiment and modify it. Try changing the message displayed on the console or adding additional statements to perform different tasks.

For example, you can modify the program to display a personalized greeting by asking the user for their name:

```
Console.WriteLine("What is your name?");
string name = Console.ReadLine();
Console.WriteLine("Hello, " + name + "!");
```

In this modified program, we use the Console.ReadLine method to read a line of text from the user and store it in the variable name. We then display a personalized greeting using the value entered by the user.

By modifying and experimenting with your program, you will gain a better understanding of the C# language and its capabilities.

Conclusion

In this section, we learned how to set up the development environment, understand the structure of a C# program, write our first C# program, and run it. We also explored how to modify the program to perform different tasks.

Now that you have a basic understanding of writing and running C# programs, we can move on to exploring variables and data types in the next chapter.

2 - Variables and Data Types

2.1 Understanding Variables

In C#, variables are used to store and manipulate data. They provide a way to give names to values and use them throughout the program. Understanding variables is essential for writing effective and efficient C# code.

2.1.1 Declaration and Initialization

Before using a variable, it needs to be declared and initialized. Declaration involves specifying the type and name of the variable, while initialization assigns an initial value to the variable. In C#, variables can be declared and initialized in a single statement or separately.

```
// Declaration and initialization in a single statement
int age = 25;
// Declaration and initialization separately
int height;
height = 180;
```

2.1.2 Variable Types

C# supports various types of variables, including primitive and non-primitive types. Primitive types are the basic building blocks of data in C#, while non-primitive types are more complex and can be created using classes or structures.

2.1.2.1 Primitive Data Types

Primitive data types in C# are predefined and include:

- **Numeric Types**: byte, sbyte, short, ushort, int, uint, long, ulong, float, double, and decimal. These types are used to store numeric values.
- **Boolean Type**: bool. This type is used to store either true or

false values.

- **Character Type**: char. This type is used to store a single character.
- **String Type**: string. This type is used to store a sequence of characters.

```
int age = 25;
bool isStudent = true;
char grade = 'A';
string name = "John Doe";
```

2.1.2.2 Non-Primitive Data Types

Non-primitive data types in C# are created using classes or structures. These types include:

- **Class Types**: Classes are reference types that can have properties, methods, and events. They are created using the class keyword.

```
class Person
{
public string Name { get; set; }
public int Age { get; set; }
}
Person person = new Person();
person.Name = "John Doe";
person.Age = 25;
```

- **Structure Types**: Structures are value types that can have properties and methods. They are created using the struct keyword.

```
struct Point
{
public int X { get; set; }
```

```
public int Y { get; set; }
}
Point point = new Point();
point.X = 10;
point.Y = 20;
```

- **Enumeration Types**: Enumerations are used to define a set of named constants. They are created using the enum keyword.

```
enum DaysOfWeek
{
Monday,
Tuesday,
Wednesday,
Thursday,
Friday,
Saturday,
Sunday
}
DaysOfWeek today = DaysOfWeek.Monday;
```

2.1.3 Variable Scope

The scope of a variable determines where it can be accessed within a program. In C#, variables can have different scopes, including:

- **Local Variables**: Local variables are declared within a method, constructor, or block of code. They are only accessible within the scope in which they are declared.

```
void PrintName()
{
string name = "John Doe";
Console.WriteLine(name);
}
```

- **Instance Variables**: Instance variables are declared within a class but outside any method. They are accessible to all methods within the class and are unique to each instance of the class.

```
class Person
{
public string Name { get; set; }
}
```

- **Static Variables**: Static variables are declared within a class but outside any method and are marked with the static keyword. They are shared among all instances of the class and can be accessed without creating an instance of the class.

```
class Counter
{
public static int Count { get; set; }
}
```

2.1.4 Variable Naming Conventions

In C#, variables should be named in a way that is meaningful and follows certain conventions. Some common naming conventions include:

- Use descriptive names that reflect the purpose of the variable.
- Start variable names with a lowercase letter.
- Use camel case for variable names (e.g., firstName, age, isStudent).
- Avoid using reserved keywords as variable names.
- Use meaningful abbreviations if necessary.

```
string firstName = "John";
int age = 25;
bool isStudent = true;
```

2.1.5 Variable Assignment and Manipulation

Variables in C# can be assigned new values and manipulated using various operators. Assignment is done using the = operator, while manipulation can be done using arithmetic, logical, and other operators.

```
int x = 10;
```

```csharp
int y = 5;
int sum = x + y; // Addition
int difference = x - y; // Subtraction
int product = x * y; // Multiplication
int quotient = x / y; // Division
int remainder = x % y; // Modulus
bool isGreater = x > y; // Greater than
bool isEqual = x == y; // Equal to
bool isNotEqual = x != y; // Not equal to
x++; // Increment
y—; // Decrement
```

Understanding variables is crucial for writing effective C# code. By knowing how to declare, initialize, and manipulate variables, you can create powerful and efficient programs.

2.2 Primitive Data Types

In C#, data types are used to define the type of data that a variable can hold. C# provides several primitive data types that are used to store simple values such as numbers, characters, and boolean values. Understanding these primitive data types is essential for writing efficient and error-free C# programs.

2.2.1 Numeric Data Types

C# provides several numeric data types to store different kinds of numbers. These include:

- **int**: The int data type is used to store whole numbers. It can hold both positive and negative values. The int data type has a size of 4 bytes and can store values ranging from -2,147,483,648 to 2,147,483,647.
- **float**: The float data type is used to store single-precision floating-point numbers. It can hold decimal values and has a size of 4 bytes. The float data type can store values with a precision of approximately 7 digits.
- **double**: The double data type is used to store double-precision floating-point numbers. It can hold decimal values and has a size of 8 bytes. The double data type can store values with a precision of approximately 15-16 digits.
- **decimal**: The decimal data type is used to store decimal numbers with high precision. It has a size of 16 bytes and can store values with a precision of approximately 28-29 digits. The decimal data type is commonly used in financial calculations where precision is crucial.

2.2.2 Character Data Types

C# provides a character data type called char to store single characters. The char data type has a size of 2 bytes and can store any Unicode character. Characters are enclosed in single quotes, such as 'A' or '5'.

2.2.3 Boolean Data Type

The boolean data type, bool, is used to store either true or false values. It is commonly used in conditional statements and logical operations. The bool data type has a size of 1 byte.

2.2.4 String Data Type

While not a primitive data type, the string data type is worth mentioning here. It is used to store a sequence of characters and is one of the most commonly used data types in C#. Strings are enclosed in double quotes, such as "Hello, World!". The string data type is immutable, meaning that once a string is created, it cannot be changed. However, you can create new strings by concatenating or manipulating existing strings.

2.2.5 Other Numeric Data Types

In addition to the numeric data types mentioned earlier, C# also provides other numeric data types with different sizes and ranges. These include:

- **byte**: The byte data type is used to store positive whole numbers ranging from 0 to 255. It has a size of 1 byte.
- **sbyte**: The sbyte data type is used to store whole numbers ranging from -128 to 127. It has a size of 1 byte.
- **short**: The short data type is used to store whole numbers ranging from -32,768 to 32,767. It has a size of 2 bytes.
- **ushort**: The ushort data type is used to store positive whole numbers ranging from 0 to 65,535. It has a size of 2 bytes.
- **long**: The long data type is used to store large whole numbers ranging from -9,223,372,036,854,775,808 to 9,223,372,036,854,775,807. It has a size of 8 bytes.

- **ulong**: The ulong data type is used to store large positive whole numbers ranging from 0 to 18,446,744,073,709,551,615. It has a size of 8 bytes.

2.2.6 Default Values

Each data type in C# has a default value, which is the value assigned to a variable if no other value is explicitly assigned. The default values for the primitive data types are as follows:

- int: 0
- float: 0.0f
- double: 0.0d
- decimal: 0.0m
- char: '\0'
- bool: false

It is important to note that variables of reference types, such as string, have a default value of null.

2.2.7 Type Conversion

In C#, you can convert one data type to another using type conversion. There are two types of type conversion: implicit and explicit.

- **Implicit Conversion**: Implicit conversion occurs when the conversion is done automatically by the compiler without the need for any explicit casting. For example, converting an int to a float is an implicit conversion because a float can hold a larger range of values than an int.
- **Explicit Conversion**: Explicit conversion, also known as casting, is done when you want to convert a value of one data type to another data type that cannot be implicitly converted. For example, converting a float to an int requires explicit

casting because an int cannot hold decimal values.

C# provides various casting operators to perform explicit type conversion, such as (int), (float), and (char).

Understanding the primitive data types in C# is crucial for writing efficient and reliable code. By choosing the appropriate data type for your variables, you can ensure that your program uses memory efficiently and avoids unnecessary type conversion errors.

2.3 Non-Primitive Data Types

In addition to primitive data types, C# also provides non-primitive data types that allow you to work with more complex and structured data. Non-primitive data types are also known as reference types because they store references to the actual data rather than the data itself. In this section, we will explore the different non-primitive data types available in C# and how to use them effectively in your programs.

2.3.1 Strings

One of the most commonly used non-primitive data types in C# is the string type. Strings are used to represent sequences of characters and are enclosed in double quotation marks. They are immutable, which means that once a string is created, it cannot be changed. However, you can create new strings by concatenating or manipulating existing strings.

```
string firstName = "John";
string lastName = "Doe";
string fullName = firstName + " " + lastName;
```

In the example above, we create three string variables: firstName, lastName, and fullName. We concatenate the firstName and lastName variables using the + operator and assign the result to the fullName variable.

Strings in C# provide a wide range of methods and properties that allow you to perform various operations on them. Some common string methods include Length, Substring, ToUpper, ToLower, Replace, and Split. These methods enable you to manipulate and extract information from strings easily.

2.3.2 Arrays

Arrays are another important non-primitive data type in C#. They allow you to store multiple values of the same type in a single variable. Arrays have a fixed length, which is determined at the time of declaration, and each element in the array is accessed using an index.

```
int[] numbers = new int[5];
numbers[0] = 1;
numbers[1] = 2;
numbers[2] = 3;
numbers[3] = 4;
numbers[4] = 5;
```

In the example above, we declare an integer array named numbers with a length of 5. We then assign values to each element of the array using the index notation. The first element is accessed using numbers[0], the second element using numbers[1], and so on.

Arrays in C# provide various methods and properties that allow you to manipulate and access their elements. Some common array methods include Length, Sort, Reverse, IndexOf, and Contains. These methods enable you to perform operations such as sorting, searching, and modifying array elements.

2.3.3 Classes

Classes are the building blocks of object-oriented programming in C#. A class is a blueprint for creating objects that encapsulate data and behavior. It defines the structure and behavior of objects of that class type. In C#, classes are reference types, which means that when you create an object of a class, you are creating a reference to the actual data.

```
public class Person
{
public string Name { get; set; }
public int Age { get; set; }
}
Person person = new Person();
person.Name = "John Doe";
person.Age = 30;
```

In the example above, we define a class named Person with two properties: Name and Age. We then create an object of the Person class and assign values to its properties.

Classes can have methods, properties, fields, and events, which allow you to define the behavior and characteristics of objects. You can also create multiple objects of the same class, each with its own set of property values.

2.3.4 Structs

Structs are similar to classes in C#, but they are value types instead of reference types. Unlike classes, which are allocated on the heap, structs are allocated on the stack. Structs are useful when you need to create lightweight objects that have value semantics.

```
public struct Point
{
public int X { get; set; }
public int Y { get; set; }
}
Point point = new Point();
point.X = 10;
point.Y = 20;
```

In the example above, we define a struct named Point with two properties: X and Y. We then create a struct object of the Point type and assign values to its properties.

Structs are commonly used to represent simple data types, such as coordinates, colors, or other small pieces of data. They are also useful when you need to pass data by value rather than by reference.

2.3.5 Enums

Enums, short for enumerations, are used to define a set of named constants. They allow you to create a custom data type with a fixed set of values. Enums are useful when you have a variable that can only take on a limited number of predefined values.

```
public enum DaysOfWeek
{
Monday,
Tuesday,
```

Wednesday,
Thursday,
Friday,
Saturday,
Sunday
}
DaysOfWeek today = DaysOfWeek.Monday;

In the example above, we define an enum named DaysOfWeek with seven named constants representing the days of the week. We then create a variable named today of the DaysOfWeek type and assign it the value Monday.

Enums in C# provide a way to improve code readability and maintainability by giving meaningful names to a set of related values.

Conclusion

Non-primitive data types in C# provide powerful ways to work with complex and structured data. Strings, arrays, classes, structs, and enums allow you to represent and manipulate different types of data in your programs. Understanding how to use these non-primitive data types effectively will greatly enhance your ability to write robust and efficient C# code.

2.4 Type Conversion and Casting

In C#, type conversion is the process of converting a value from one data type to another. This is necessary when you want to assign a value of one data type to a variable of a different data type, or when you want to perform operations on values of different data types. C# provides several ways to perform type conversion, including implicit conversion, explicit conversion, and casting.

2.4.1 Implicit Conversion

Implicit conversion, also known as widening conversion, is the automatic conversion of a value from one data type to another without the need for any explicit casting or conversion functions. This conversion is possible when there is no risk of data loss or precision loss. For example, converting an integer to a floating-point number or assigning a smaller data type to a larger data type.

Here's an example of implicit conversion:

int num = 10;

double decimalNum = num; // Implicit conversion from int to double

In this example, the integer value 10 is implicitly converted to a double value 10.0 because there is no risk of data loss.

2.4.2 Explicit Conversion

Explicit conversion, also known as narrowing conversion, is the manual conversion of a value from one data type to another using casting or conversion functions. This conversion is necessary when there is a risk of data loss or precision loss. For example, converting a floating-point number to an integer or assigning a larger data type to a smaller data type.

Here's an example of explicit conversion using casting:

double decimalNum = 10.5;

int num = (int)decimalNum; // Explicit conversion using casting

In this example, the double value 10.5 is explicitly converted to an integer value 10 using casting. It's important to note that explicit conversion may result in data loss or truncation of the value.

2.4.3 Boxing and Unboxing

Boxing and unboxing are the processes of converting a value type to a reference type and vice versa. In C#, value types are stored on the stack, while reference types are stored on the heap. Boxing allows you to treat a value type as an object, while unboxing allows you to extract the value type from an object.

Here's an example of boxing and unboxing:

```
int num = 10;
object boxedNum = num; // Boxing - converting int to object
int unboxedNum = (int)boxedNum; // Unboxing - converting object to int
```

In this example, the integer value 10 is boxed into an object, allowing it to be treated as a reference type. Later, the value is unboxed and assigned back to an integer variable.

2.4.4 Conversion Functions

C# provides several built-in conversion functions that allow you to convert values between different data types. These functions include Convert.ToXxx, Parse, and TryParse.

The Convert.ToXxx functions are used to convert a value to a specific data type. For example, Convert.ToInt32 converts a value to an integer, Convert.ToDouble converts a value to a double, and so on.

The Parse function is used to convert a string representation of a value to the corresponding data type. For example, int.Parse converts a string to an integer, double.Parse converts a string to a double, and so on.

The TryParse function is similar to Parse, but it returns a boolean value indicating whether the conversion was successful or not. This function is useful when you want to handle conversion errors without throwing an exception.

Here's an example of using conversion functions:

```
string numString = "10";
int num = int.Parse(numString); // Parsing a string to an integer
double decimalNum;
bool success = double.TryParse(numString, out decimalNum); // Trying to parse a string to a double
```

In this example, the string value "10" is parsed to an integer using int.Parse. The TryParse function is used to parse the same string to a double, and the result is stored in the decimalNum variable. The success variable indicates whether the conversion was successful or not.

2.4.5 User-Defined Type Conversion

In addition to the built-in type conversion mechanisms, C# also allows you to define your own type conversions using user-defined conversion operators. These operators enable you to define how an object of one type can be converted to another type.

User-defined type conversion operators are defined as static methods in a class and must be explicitly invoked. They can be used to convert between custom types or to provide custom conversion behavior for built-in types.

Here's an example of a user-defined type conversion:

```
class Distance
{
public double Meters { get; set; }
public static explicit operator double(Distance distance)
{
return distance.Meters;
}
public static implicit operator Distance(double meters)
{
return new Distance { Meters = meters };
}
}
```

Distance distance = new Distance { Meters = 10.5 };

double   meters   =   (double)distance;   //   Explicit   user-defined conversion

Distance newDistance = 20.5; // Implicit user-defined conversion

In this example, the Distance class defines both explicit and implicit conversion operators. The explicit operator allows converting a Distance object to a double, while the implicit operator allows converting a double to a Distance object. These operators can be used to convert between Distance objects and double values.

Conclusion

Type conversion and casting are essential concepts in C# programming. They allow you to convert values between different data types, enabling you to perform operations and assignments with ease. Understanding the different types of conversion and when to use them is crucial for writing efficient and error-free code.

3 - Control Flow

3.1 Conditional Statements

Conditional statements are an essential part of any programming language, including C#. They allow you to control the flow of your program based on certain conditions. In this section, we will explore the different types of conditional statements available in C# and how to use them effectively.

3.1.1 If Statement

The if statement is the most basic form of a conditional statement in C#. It allows you to execute a block of code only if a certain condition is true. The syntax of the if statement is as follows:

```
if (condition)
{
// code to be executed if the condition is true
}
```

The condition inside the parentheses must evaluate to a boolean value (true or false). If the condition is true, the code inside the curly braces will be executed. If the condition is false, the code block will be skipped.

Here's an example to illustrate the usage of the if statement:

```
int x = 10;
if (x > 5)
{
Console.WriteLine("x is greater than 5");
}
```

In this example, the condition x > 5 evaluates to true because the value of x is 10, which is indeed greater than 5. Therefore, the code inside the if block will be executed, and the message "x is greater than 5" will be printed to the console.

3.1.2 If-Else Statement

The if-else statement allows you to execute different blocks of code based on the result of a condition. If the condition is true, the code inside the if block will be executed. If the condition is false, the code inside the else block will be executed. The syntax of the if-else statement is as follows:

```
if (condition)
{
// code to be executed if the condition is true
}
else
{
// code to be executed if the condition is false
}
```

Here's an example to illustrate the usage of the if-else statement:

```
int x = 10;
if (x > 5)
{
Console.WriteLine("x is greater than 5");
}
else
{
Console.WriteLine("x is less than or equal to 5");
}
```

In this example, the condition x > 5 evaluates to true, so the code inside the if block will be executed, and the message "x is greater than 5" will be printed to the console.

3.1.3 Nested If Statements

Nested if statements allow you to have multiple levels of conditions within your code. You can have an if statement inside another if statement. This allows for more complex decision-making processes. Here's an example:

```
int x = 10;
int y = 5;
if (x > 5)
```

```
{
if (y > 2)
{
Console.WriteLine("Both x and y are greater than their respective
thresholds");
}
else
{
Console.WriteLine("x is greater than 5, but y is not greater than
2");
}
}
else
{
Console.WriteLine("x is not greater than 5");
}
```

In this example, the outer if statement checks if x is greater than 5. If it is, the inner if statement checks if y is greater than 2. If both conditions are true, the message "Both x and y are greater than their respective thresholds" will be printed. If the outer condition is true but the inner condition is false, the message "x is greater than 5, but y is not greater than 2" will be printed. If the outer condition is false, the message "x is not greater than 5" will be printed.

3.1.4 Switch Statement

The switch statement provides an alternative way to handle multiple conditions. It allows you to specify different cases and execute code based on the value of a variable. The syntax of the switch statement is as follows:

```
switch (variable)
{
case value1:
// code to be executed if variable equals value1
```

```
break;
case value2:
// code to be executed if variable equals value2
break;
default:
// code to be executed if variable does not match any case
break;
}
```

Here's an example to illustrate the usage of the switch statement:

```
int day = 3;
switch (day)
{
case 1:
Console.WriteLine("Monday");
break;
case 2:
Console.WriteLine("Tuesday");
break;
case 3:
Console.WriteLine("Wednesday");
break;
default:
Console.WriteLine("Invalid day");
break;
}
```

In this example, the variable day is set to 3. The switch statement checks the value of day and executes the code block corresponding to the matching case. In this case, the message "Wednesday" will be printed to the console.

3.1.5 Ternary Operator

The ternary operator is a shorthand way of writing an if-else statement in a single line. It allows you to assign a value to a variable based on a condition. The syntax of the ternary operator is as follows:

variable = (condition) ? value1 : value2;

If the condition is true, value1 will be assigned to variable. If the condition is false, value2 will be assigned to variable.

Here's an example to illustrate the usage of the ternary operator:

int x = 10;

int y = (x > 5) ? 1 : 2;

In this example, the condition x > 5 evaluates to true, so the value 1 will be assigned to y.

Conditional statements are powerful tools that allow you to make decisions and control the flow of your program. By understanding and utilizing the different types of conditional statements available in C#, you can write more efficient and flexible code.

3.2 Loops

Loops are an essential part of any programming language, including C#. They allow you to repeat a block of code multiple times, making it easier to perform repetitive tasks or iterate over collections of data. In this section, we will explore the different types of loops available in C# and learn how to use them effectively.

3.2.1 The for Loop

The for loop is one of the most commonly used loops in C#. It allows you to specify the initialization, condition, and iteration statements all in one line. Here's the basic syntax of a for loop:

```
for (initialization; condition; iteration)
{
// code to be executed
}
```

Let's break down each part of the for loop:

- Initialization: This statement is executed only once before the loop starts. It is used to initialize the loop control variable.
- Condition: This statement is evaluated before each iteration. If the condition is true, the loop continues; otherwise, it terminates.
- Iteration: This statement is executed after each iteration. It is used to update the loop control variable.

Here's an example that demonstrates the usage of a for loop:

```
for (int i = 0; i < 5; i++)
{
Console.WriteLine("Iteration: " + i);
}
```

In this example, the loop will iterate five times, starting from 0 and incrementing i by 1 after each iteration. The output will be:

Iteration: 0

Iteration: 1

Iteration: 2

Iteration: 3

Iteration: 4

3.2.2 The while Loop

The while loop is another type of loop in C#. It repeats a block of code as long as a specified condition is true. Here's the basic syntax of a while loop:

```
while (condition)
{
// code to be executed
}
```

The condition is evaluated before each iteration. If the condition is true, the loop continues; otherwise, it terminates. Here's an example that demonstrates the usage of a while loop:

```
int i = 0;
while (i < 5)
{
Console.WriteLine("Iteration: " + i);
i++;
}
```

In this example, the loop will iterate five times, starting from 0 and incrementing i by 1 after each iteration. The output will be the same as the for loop example.

3.2.3 The do-while Loop

The do-while loop is similar to the while loop, but it guarantees that the code block is executed at least once, even if the condition is false. Here's the basic syntax of a do-while loop:

```
do
{
// code to be executed
```

} while (condition);

The code block is executed first, and then the condition is evaluated. If the condition is true, the loop continues; otherwise, it terminates. Here's an example that demonstrates the usage of a do-while loop:

```
int i = 0;
do
{
Console.WriteLine("Iteration: " + i);
i++;
} while (i < 5);
```

In this example, the loop will iterate five times, starting from 0 and incrementing i by 1 after each iteration. The output will be the same as the previous examples.

3.2.4 The foreach Loop

The foreach loop is specifically designed for iterating over collections, such as arrays or lists. It simplifies the process of accessing each element in the collection without the need for an index variable. Here's the basic syntax of a foreach loop:

```
foreach (type variable in collection)
{
// code to be executed
}
```

The type represents the type of elements in the collection, and the variable is a temporary variable that holds each element during iteration. Here's an example that demonstrates the usage of a foreach loop:

```
int[] numbers = { 1, 2, 3, 4, 5 };
foreach (int number in numbers)
{
Console.WriteLine("Number: " + number);
}
```

In this example, the loop will iterate over each element in the numbers array and print its value. The output will be:

Number: 1

Number: 2

Number: 3

Number: 4

Number: 5

3.2.5 Loop Control Statements

C# provides several loop control statements that allow you to control the flow of execution within a loop. These statements include break, continue, and goto.

- The break statement is used to terminate the loop prematurely. When encountered, it immediately exits the loop and continues with the next statement after the loop.
- The continue statement is used to skip the rest of the current iteration and move to the next iteration of the loop.
- The goto statement is used to transfer control to a labeled statement within the same method. However, the usage of goto is generally discouraged as it can make the code harder to read and understand.

It's important to use these loop control statements judiciously to avoid creating complex and hard-to-maintain code.

Conclusion

Loops are powerful constructs that allow you to repeat a block of code multiple times. In this section, we explored the different types of loops available in C#, including the for, while, do-while, and foreach loops. We also learned about loop control statements that help control the flow of execution within a loop. By mastering loops, you can write more efficient and concise code in C#.

3.3 Switch Statements

In C#, the switch statement is a powerful control flow statement that allows you to execute different blocks of code based on the value of a variable or an expression. It provides a concise and efficient way to handle multiple conditions without the need for multiple if-else statements.

Syntax

The syntax of a switch statement in C# is as follows:

```
switch (expression)
{
case value1:
// code to be executed if expression matches value1
break;
case value2:
// code to be executed if expression matches value2
break;
case value3:
// code to be executed if expression matches value3
break;
// more cases...
default:
// code to be executed if expression doesn't match any case
break;
}
```

The switch statement starts with the keyword switch, followed by the expression in parentheses. The expression can be of any data type that is compatible with the equality operator (==). Inside the switch block, you define different cases using the case keyword, followed by a value that the expression will be compared against. If the expression matches a case, the corresponding block of code will be executed. The break statement is used to exit the switch block and prevent the execution of subsequent cases. The default case is optional and is executed if none of the cases match the expression.

Working with Switch Statements

Switch statements are commonly used when you have a variable or an expression that can take on multiple values, and you want to perform different actions based on those values. Let's consider an example where we want to display a message based on the day of the week:

```
int dayOfWeek = 3;
string message;
switch (dayOfWeek)
{
case 1:
message = "Today is Monday";
break;
case 2:
message = "Today is Tuesday";
break;
case 3:
message = "Today is Wednesday";
break;
case 4:
message = "Today is Thursday";
break;
case 5:
message = "Today is Friday";
break;
case 6:
message = "Today is Saturday";
break;
case 7:
message = "Today is Sunday";
```

```
break;
default:
message = "Invalid day of the week";
break;
}
Console.WriteLine(message);
```

In this example, the variable dayOfWeek is set to 3, which corresponds to Wednesday. The switch statement compares the value of dayOfWeek against each case, and when it finds a match, it assigns the corresponding message to the message variable. In this case, the output will be "Today is Wednesday".

If the value of dayOfWeek doesn't match any of the cases, the default case will be executed, and the message "Invalid day of the week" will be assigned to message.

Fall-Through Behavior

By default, each case in a switch statement is independent, meaning that once a case is matched and executed, the switch block is exited. However, there are cases where you might want to execute multiple cases sequentially. This behavior is known as fall-through.

To achieve fall-through behavior, you can omit the break statement at the end of a case. When the code execution reaches the end of a case without a break statement, it will continue to the next case without checking its condition. Here's an example:

```
int number = 2;
switch (number)
{
case 1:
Console.WriteLine("One");
break;
case 2:
Console.WriteLine("Two");
// fall-through to the next case
```

```
case 3:
Console.WriteLine("Three");
break;
default:
Console.WriteLine("Invalid number");
break;
}
```

In this example, when number is 2, the output will be:

Two

Three

Since there is no break statement after the "Two" case, the code execution falls through to the "Three" case, and both messages are printed.

Switch Statement vs. If-Else Statement

Switch statements are often used as an alternative to if-else statements when you have multiple conditions to check. They provide a more concise and readable way to handle multiple cases. However, there are some differences between switch statements and if-else statements that you should be aware of.

- Switch statements can only be used to compare a single expression against multiple values, whereas if-else statements can handle more complex conditions involving multiple expressions.

- Switch statements are generally more efficient than if-else statements when there are many cases to check, as they use a jump table to quickly determine the appropriate code block to execute.

- If-else statements allow for more flexibility in terms of condition evaluation, as you can use logical operators (&&, ||, etc.) to combine multiple conditions.

In general, switch statements are a great choice when you have a single expression to compare against multiple values, and if-else statements are better suited for more complex conditions involving multiple expressions.

Conclusion

Switch statements provide a powerful and efficient way to handle multiple conditions in C#. They allow you to execute different blocks of code based on the value of a variable or an expression. By using switch statements effectively, you can write cleaner and more readable code.

3.4 Exception Handling

Exception handling is an essential aspect of any programming language, including C#. It allows developers to handle and manage unexpected errors or exceptional situations that may occur during the execution of a program. By implementing exception handling, you can gracefully handle errors, prevent program crashes, and provide meaningful feedback to users.

3.4.1 Understanding Exceptions

In C#, an exception is an object that represents an error or an exceptional condition that occurs during the execution of a program. When an exceptional situation arises, the program throws an exception, which can be caught and handled by the appropriate exception handling code.

Exceptions can occur due to various reasons, such as invalid input, file not found, network errors, or arithmetic errors. C# provides a wide range of built-in exception classes that cover different types of errors. These exception classes are organized in a hierarchy, with the base class being System.Exception.

3.4.2 Try-Catch-Finally

The try-catch-finally block is the primary mechanism for handling exceptions in C#. The try block contains the code that may throw an exception. If an exception occurs within the try block, the program jumps to the corresponding catch block.

The catch block specifies the type of exception it can handle. When an exception of that type is thrown, the code within the catch block is executed. Multiple catch blocks can be used to handle different types of exceptions.

```
try
{
// Code that may throw an exception
}
```

```
catch (ExceptionType1 ex)
{
// Exception handling code for ExceptionType1
}
catch (ExceptionType2 ex)
{
// Exception handling code for ExceptionType2
}
finally
{
// Code that always executes, regardless of whether an exception
occurred or not
}
```

The finally block is optional and is used to specify code that should always execute, regardless of whether an exception occurred or not. It is commonly used for cleanup operations, such as closing files or releasing resources.

3.4.3 Throwing Exceptions

In addition to handling exceptions, C# also allows you to explicitly throw exceptions using the throw keyword. This is useful when you want to indicate an exceptional condition in your code.

```
if (condition)
{
throw new Exception("An exceptional condition occurred.");
}
```

By throwing an exception, you can interrupt the normal flow of the program and transfer control to the nearest catch block that can handle the exception.

3.4.4 Custom Exceptions

While C# provides a wide range of built-in exception classes, you can also create your own custom exception classes to handle specific exceptional conditions in your code. Custom exceptions can be derived from the base class System.Exception or any of its derived classes.

To create a custom exception class, you need to define a new class and inherit from the appropriate base class. You can then add any additional properties or methods that are relevant to your specific exception.

```
public class CustomException : Exception
{
public CustomException(string message) : base(message)
{
// Additional initialization code
}
}
```

Once you have defined your custom exception class, you can throw instances of it using the throw keyword, and handle them using the catch block.

```
try
{
if (condition)
{
throw new CustomException("An exceptional condition occurred.");
}
}
catch (CustomException ex)
{
// Exception handling code for CustomException
}
```

Custom exceptions allow you to provide more specific and meaningful error messages to users and handle exceptional conditions in a more granular manner.

Exception handling is a crucial aspect of writing robust and reliable code in C#. By understanding how to handle exceptions, you can ensure that your programs gracefully handle errors and provide a better user experience.

3.5 Jump Statements

Jump statements in C# allow you to alter the normal flow of control in a program. They provide a way to transfer control to a different part of the program, skipping over certain sections of code or repeating sections multiple times. In this section, we will explore the different types of jump statements available in C# and how to use them effectively in your programs.

3.5.1 The break Statement

The break statement is commonly used in loops and switch statements to exit the loop or switch block prematurely. When encountered, the break statement immediately terminates the innermost loop or switch block and transfers control to the next statement after the loop or switch block.

Let's consider an example where we want to find the first occurrence of a specific number in an array:

```
int[] numbers = { 1, 2, 3, 4, 5, 6, 7, 8, 9, 10 };
int target = 6;
foreach (int number in numbers)
{
if (number == target)
{
Console.WriteLine("Target found!");
break;
}
}
```

In this example, the break statement is used to exit the loop as soon as the target number is found. Without the break statement, the loop would continue iterating through the remaining numbers even after finding the target.

3.5.2 The continue Statement

The continue statement is used to skip the rest of the current iteration of a loop and move on to the next iteration. When encountered, the continue statement immediately transfers control to the loop condition or the next iteration of the loop.

Let's consider an example where we want to print all the even numbers in a given range:

```
for (int i = 1; i <= 10; i++)
{
if (i % 2 != 0)
{
continue;
}
Console.WriteLine(i);
}
```

In this example, the continue statement is used to skip the odd numbers and move on to the next iteration of the loop. As a result, only the even numbers from 1 to 10 will be printed.

3.5.3 The goto Statement

The goto statement allows you to transfer control to a labeled statement within the same method. It is often considered a controversial statement and should be used sparingly, as it can make code harder to read and understand.

Here's an example that demonstrates the usage of the goto statement:

```
int count = 0;
start:
count++;
if (count < 10)
{
goto start;
}
Console.WriteLine("Count: " + count);
```

In this example, the goto statement is used to transfer control back to the start label, incrementing the count variable until it reaches 10. Once the condition is no longer satisfied, the program continues executing from the statement after the goto statement.

3.5.4 The return Statement

The return statement is used to exit a method and return a value, if specified, to the calling code. When encountered, the return statement immediately terminates the execution of the current method and transfers control back to the calling code.

Here's an example that demonstrates the usage of the return statement:

```
int Add(int a, int b)
{
return a + b;
}
int result = Add(5, 3);
Console.WriteLine("Result: " + result);
```

In this example, the return statement is used to exit the Add method and return the sum of the two input parameters. The returned value is then assigned to the result variable and printed to the console.

3.5.5 The **throw** Statement

The throw statement is used to explicitly throw an exception in C#. It allows you to create custom exceptions or rethrow existing exceptions. When encountered, the throw statement immediately transfers control to the nearest catch block that can handle the thrown exception.

Here's an example that demonstrates the usage of the throw statement:

```
void Divide(int a, int b)
{
if (b == 0)
{
```

```
throw new DivideByZeroException("Cannot divide by zero.");
}
int result = a / b;
Console.WriteLine("Result: " + result);
}
try
{
Divide(10, 0);
}
catch (DivideByZeroException ex)
{
Console.WriteLine("Error: " + ex.Message);
}
```

In this example, the throw statement is used to throw a DivideByZeroException when the second parameter of the Divide method is zero. The thrown exception is then caught in the catch block, allowing us to handle the error gracefully.

Conclusion

Jump statements provide powerful control flow mechanisms in C# that allow you to alter the normal execution of your programs. The break statement allows you to exit loops and switch statements prematurely, while the continue statement allows you to skip the rest of the current iteration of a loop. The goto statement, although controversial, allows you to transfer control to a labeled statement within the same method. The return statement allows you to exit a method and return a value to the calling code, and the throw statement allows you to explicitly throw exceptions. Understanding and using these jump statements effectively will enhance your ability to write efficient and flexible C# programs.

4 - Arrays and Collections

4.1 Arrays

In C#, an array is a data structure that allows you to store multiple values of the same type in a single variable. Arrays are useful when you need to work with a collection of elements that share a common characteristic or when you want to access elements by their index.

4.1.1 Declaring and Initializing Arrays

To declare an array in C#, you need to specify the type of the elements it will hold, followed by square brackets [] and the name of the array variable. Here's an example:

int[] numbers;

In this example, we declare an array called "numbers" that can hold integers. However, at this point, the array is uninitialized, meaning it doesn't have any elements.

To initialize an array, you can use the "new" keyword followed by the type of the elements and the number of elements you want the array to hold. Here's an example:

int[] numbers = new int[5];

In this example, we initialize the "numbers" array to hold 5 integers. The array is now ready to be used, and all elements are set to their default values (0 in the case of integers).

Alternatively, you can also initialize an array with specific values using an array initializer. Here's an example:

int[] numbers = { 1, 2, 3, 4, 5 };

In this example, we initialize the "numbers" array with the values 1, 2, 3, 4, and 5. The size of the array is automatically determined based on the number of values provided.

4.1.2 Accessing Array Elements

Array elements are accessed using their index, which starts at 0 for the first element and increments by 1 for each subsequent element. To access an element, you need to specify the array variable name followed by the index in square brackets. Here's an example:

int[] numbers = { 1, 2, 3, 4, 5 };

int firstNumber = numbers[0]; // Accessing the first element

int thirdNumber = numbers[2]; // Accessing the third element

In this example, we access the first element of the "numbers" array and assign it to the variable "firstNumber". We also access the third element and assign it to the variable "thirdNumber".

It's important to note that accessing an element outside the bounds of the array will result in an "IndexOutOfRangeException" at runtime. Therefore, you should always ensure that the index is within the valid range of the array.

4.1.3 Modifying Array Elements

Once an array is initialized, you can modify its elements by assigning new values to them. To modify an element, you need to specify the array variable name followed by the index in square brackets and assign the new value. Here's an example:

int[] numbers = { 1, 2, 3, 4, 5 };

numbers[0] = 10; // Modifying the first element

numbers[2] = 30; // Modifying the third element

In this example, we modify the value of the first element of the "numbers" array to 10 and the value of the third element to 30.

4.1.4 Array Length

The length of an array represents the number of elements it can hold. In C#, you can get the length of an array using the "Length" property. Here's an example:

int[] numbers = { 1, 2, 3, 4, 5 };

int length = numbers.Length; // Getting the length of the array

In this example, we get the length of the "numbers" array and assign it to the variable "length". The value of "length" will be 5, as the array can hold 5 elements.

4.1.5 Multidimensional Arrays

In addition to single-dimensional arrays, C# also supports multidimensional arrays. A multidimensional array is an array that contains multiple arrays, forming a matrix-like structure.

To declare a multidimensional array, you need to specify the type of the elements it will hold, followed by multiple sets of square brackets [] and the name of the array variable. Here's an example:

int[,] matrix;

In this example, we declare a two-dimensional array called "matrix" that can hold integers. However, at this point, the array is uninitialized.

To initialize a multidimensional array, you can use the "new" keyword followed by the type of the elements and the dimensions of the array. Here's an example:

int[,] matrix = new int[3, 3];

In this example, we initialize the "matrix" array to hold 3 rows and 3 columns of integers. The array is now ready to be used, and all elements are set to their default values (0 in the case of integers).

You can access and modify elements of a multidimensional array using multiple indices. Here's an example:

int[,] matrix = new int[3, 3];

matrix[0, 0] = 1; // Accessing and modifying the element at row 0, column 0

matrix[1, 2] = 3; // Accessing and modifying the element at row 1, column 2

In this example, we access and modify the element at row 0, column 0 of the "matrix" array, and the element at row 1, column 2.

4.1.6 Jagged Arrays

In addition to multidimensional arrays, C# also supports jagged arrays. A jagged array is an array of arrays, where each element can be an array of different lengths.

To declare a jagged array, you need to specify the type of the elements it will hold, followed by a set of square brackets [] and the name of the array variable. Here's an example:

int[][] jaggedArray;

In this example, we declare a jagged array called "jaggedArray" that can hold arrays of integers. However, at this point, the array is uninitialized.

To initialize a jagged array, you can use the "new" keyword followed by the type of the elements and the number of arrays you want the jagged array to hold. Here's an example:

int[][] jaggedArray = new int[3][];

In this example, we initialize the "jaggedArray" to hold 3 arrays of integers. The array is now ready to be used, but each element is still uninitialized.

To initialize the individual arrays within the jagged array, you can use the "new" keyword followed by the type of the elements and the number of elements you want each array to hold. Here's an example:

```
int[][] jaggedArray = new int[3][];
jaggedArray[0] = new int[2];
jaggedArray[1] = new int[3];
jaggedArray[2] = new int[4];
```

In this example, we initialize the first array within the "jaggedArray" to hold 2 integers, the second array to hold 3 integers, and the third array to hold 4 integers.

You can access and modify elements of a jagged array using multiple indices. Here's an example:

```
int[][] jaggedArray = new int[3][];
jaggedArray[0] = new int[2];
jaggedArray[1] = new int[3];
jaggedArray[2] = new int[4];
jaggedArray[0][0] = 1; // Accessing and modifying the element at
index 0 of the first array
jaggedArray[1][2] = 3; // Accessing and modifying the element at
index 2 of the second array
```

In this example, we access and modify the element at index 0 of the first array within the "jaggedArray" and the element at index 2 of the second array.

4.1.7 Array Methods and Properties

C# provides several methods and properties that you can use to work with arrays. Here are some commonly used ones:

- **Array.Sort()**: Sorts the elements of an array in ascending order.
- **Array.Reverse()**: Reverses the order of the elements in an array.
- **Array.Copy()**: Copies a range of elements from one array to another.
- **Array.IndexOf()**: Searches for the specified element in an array and returns its index.
- **Array.Contains()**: Determines whether an array contains a specific element and returns a boolean value.
- **Array.Length**: Gets the number of elements in an array.

These methods and properties can be useful when you need to perform common operations on arrays, such as sorting, searching, or copying elements.

Conclusion

Arrays are a fundamental data structure in C# that allow you to store and manipulate collections of elements. They provide a convenient way to work with multiple values of the same type and offer various methods and properties for performing common operations. Understanding how to declare, initialize, access, and modify arrays is essential for mastering C# programming.

4.2 Lists

In this section, we will explore the concept of lists in C#. Lists are a fundamental data structure that allows you to store and manipulate collections of objects. Unlike arrays, lists are dynamic in size, meaning you can add or remove elements as needed. Lists provide a flexible and efficient way to work with collections of data in your C# programs.

4.2.1 Introduction to Lists

A list is a generic collection class provided by the .NET framework. It is defined in the System.Collections.Generic namespace. Lists can store elements of any type, including both value types and reference types. To create a list, you need to specify the type of elements it will store. For example, to create a list of integers, you would use the following code:

```
List<int> numbers = new List<int>();
```

In this example, we create an empty list of integers named numbers. The <int> part specifies the type of elements the list will store. You can replace int with any other valid C# type.

4.2.2 Adding and Removing Elements

Lists provide several methods to add and remove elements. The most commonly used methods are Add, Remove, and RemoveAt.

To add an element to the end of the list, you can use the Add method. For example:

```
numbers.Add(10);
numbers.Add(20);
numbers.Add(30);
```

In this example, we add three integers to the numbers list.

To remove an element from the list, you can use the Remove method. This method removes the first occurrence of the specified element. For example:

```
numbers.Remove(20);
```

In this cxample, we remove the number 20 from the numbers list.

If you know the index of the element you want to remove, you can use the RemoveAt method. This method removes the element at the specified index. For example:

numbers.RemoveAt(0);

In this example, we remove the first element from the numbers list.

4.2.3 Accessing Elements

Lists provide several ways to access elements. The most commonly used methods are indexing and iteration.

To access an element at a specific index, you can use the indexing operator []. For example:

int firstNumber = numbers[0];

In this example, we retrieve the first element from the numbers list.

Lists also provide a property called Count that returns the number of elements in the list. You can use this property in conjunction with a loop to iterate over all the elements in the list. For example:

```
for (int i = 0; i < numbers.Count; i++)
{
Console.WriteLine(numbers[i]);
}
```

In this example, we use a for loop to iterate over all the elements in the numbers list and print them to the console.

4.2.4 List Methods and Properties

Lists provide a wide range of methods and properties to manipulate and query the elements. Some of the commonly used methods and properties are:

- AddRange: Adds the elements of another collection to the end of the list.
- Clear: Removes all elements from the list.
- Contains: Determines whether the list contains a specific element.
- IndexOf: Returns the index of the first occurrence of a specific element.

- Insert: Inserts an element at the specified index.
- Sort: Sorts the elements in the list.
- ToArray: Converts the list to an array.

These are just a few examples of the methods and properties available in the List class. You can refer to the official Microsoft documentation for a complete list of methods and properties.

4.2.5 List Initialization

In addition to adding elements one by one, you can also initialize a list with a collection of elements using collection initializer syntax. For example:

List<int> numbers = new List<int> { 10, 20, 30 };

In this example, we create a list of integers named numbers and initialize it with three elements.

4.2.6 List Performance

Lists provide efficient performance for most operations. Adding and removing elements at the end of the list is a constant time operation. However, adding or removing elements at the beginning or middle of the list requires shifting the existing elements, which can be an expensive operation for large lists.

When working with large lists, consider using other data structures such as LinkedList or HashSet if the performance of adding or removing elements at arbitrary positions is critical.

4.2.7 Summary

In this section, we explored the concept of lists in C#. Lists are dynamic collections that allow you to store and manipulate elements of any type. We learned how to add and remove elements, access elements using indexing and iteration, and use various methods and properties provided by the List class. We also discussed list initialization and performance considerations. Lists are a powerful tool in C# programming and can greatly simplify working with collections of data.

4.3 Dictionaries

In this section, we will explore the concept of dictionaries in C#. Dictionaries are a powerful data structure that allows you to store and retrieve key-value pairs. They provide a fast and efficient way to look up values based on their associated keys.

4.3.1 Introduction to Dictionaries

A dictionary is a collection of key-value pairs, where each key is unique within the collection. The keys are used to access the corresponding values. Dictionaries are commonly used when you need to quickly retrieve values based on a specific key, rather than iterating over the entire collection.

In C#, dictionaries are implemented using the Dictionary<TKey, TValue> class from the System.Collections.Generic namespace. The TKey type represents the type of the keys, and the TValue type represents the type of the values.

4.3.2 Creating and Initializing Dictionaries

To create a dictionary, you can use the following syntax:

Dictionary<TKey, TValue> dictionary = new Dictionary<TKey, TValue>();

Here, TKey and TValue are the types of the keys and values, respectively. You can replace TKey and TValue with the actual types you want to use.

You can also initialize a dictionary with some initial key-value pairs using the collection initializer syntax:

Dictionary<string, int> ages = new Dictionary<string, int>()
{
{ "John", 25 },
{ "Jane", 30 },
{ "Mike", 35 }
};

In this example, we create a dictionary called ages with keys of type string and values of type int. We initialize it with three key-value pairs.

4.3.3 Adding and Accessing Elements in a Dictionary

To add elements to a dictionary, you can use the Add method:

dictionary.Add(key, value);

Here, key is the key of the element, and value is the value associated with the key.

To access the value associated with a specific key, you can use the indexer syntax:

TValue value = dictionary[key];

Here, key is the key of the element, and value is the value associated with the key.

4.3.4 Modifying and Removing Elements in a Dictionary

To modify the value associated with a specific key, you can use the indexer syntax:

dictionary[key] = newValue;

Here, key is the key of the element, and newValue is the new value to be associated with the key.

To remove an element from a dictionary, you can use the Remove method:

dictionary.Remove(key);

Here, key is the key of the element to be removed.

4.3.5 Checking if a Dictionary Contains a Key

To check if a dictionary contains a specific key, you can use the ContainsKey method:

bool containsKey = dictionary.ContainsKey(key);

Here, key is the key to be checked, and containsKey is a boolean variable that indicates whether the dictionary contains the key or not.

4.3.6 Enumerating Elements in a Dictionary

There are several ways to enumerate the elements in a dictionary. One common way is to use a foreach loop:

foreach (KeyValuePair<TKey, TValue> pair in dictionary)

```
{
TKey key = pair.Key;
TValue value = pair.Value;
// Do something with the key and value
}
```

Here, KeyValuePair<TKey, TValue> is a struct that represents a key-value pair in the dictionary. The Key property gives you the key, and the Value property gives you the value.

Another way to enumerate the elements is to use the Keys or Values property of the dictionary:

```
foreach (TKey key in dictionary.Keys)
{
TValue value = dictionary[key];
// Do something with the key and value
}
```

In this example, we iterate over the keys of the dictionary and use each key to access the corresponding value.

4.3.7 Dictionary Methods and Properties

The Dictionary<TKey, TValue> class provides several useful methods and properties to work with dictionaries. Some of the commonly used ones include:

- Count: Gets the number of key-value pairs in the dictionary.
- Clear: Removes all key-value pairs from the dictionary.
- TryGetValue: Tries to get the value associated with a specific key, without throwing an exception if the key is not found.
- Keys: Gets a collection containing all the keys in the dictionary.
- Values: Gets a collection containing all the values in the dictionary.

These methods and properties can be used to perform various operations on dictionaries, such as counting the number of elements, clearing the dictionary, or retrieving all the keys or values.

4.3.8 Summary

Dictionaries are a powerful data structure in C# that allow you to store and retrieve key-value pairs efficiently. They are commonly used when you need to quickly look up values based on specific keys. In this section, we covered the basics of dictionaries, including creating and initializing dictionaries, adding and accessing elements, modifying and removing elements, checking if a dictionary contains a key, and enumerating elements. We also explored some of the useful methods and properties provided by the Dictionary<TKey, TValue> class.

4.4 Sets

In this section, we will explore the concept of sets in C#. A set is a collection of unique elements, where each element occurs only once. Sets are useful when you need to work with a collection of items without any duplicates. In C#, sets are implemented using the HashSet<T> class from the System.Collections.Generic namespace.

4.4.1 Introduction to Sets

A set is an unordered collection of elements that does not allow duplicate values. It is similar to a mathematical set, where each element is unique and the order of elements does not matter. Sets are commonly used in scenarios where you need to perform operations such as union, intersection, and difference on collections.

In C#, the HashSet<T> class provides an efficient way to work with sets. It uses a hash table internally to store the elements, which allows for fast insertion, deletion, and lookup operations. The HashSet<T> class is part of the .NET Framework and is available in all versions of C#.

4.4.2 Creating a Set

To create a set in C#, you need to instantiate an object of the HashSet<T> class. The type parameter T specifies the type of elements that the set will contain. For example, to create a set of integers, you can use the following code:

HashSet<int> numbers = new HashSet<int>();

This creates an empty set of integers. You can also initialize a set with a collection of elements using the collection initializer syntax. For example:

HashSet<int> numbers = new HashSet<int> { 1, 2, 3, 4, 5 };

This creates a set of integers with the elements 1, 2, 3, 4, and 5.

4.4.3 Adding and Removing Elements

To add an element to a set, you can use the Add method of the HashSet<T> class. The Add method returns a boolean value indicating whether the element was successfully added to the set. If the element is already present in the set, it will not be added again. For example:

HashSet<int> numbers = new HashSet<int>();

numbers.Add(1); // Adds the element 1 to the set

numbers.Add(2); // Adds the element 2 to the set

numbers.Add(1); // Does not add the element 1 again, as it is already present in the set

To remove an element from a set, you can use the Remove method. The Remove method returns a boolean value indicating whether the element was successfully removed from the set. If the element is not present in the set, it will not be removed. For example:

HashSet<int> numbers = new HashSet<int> { 1, 2, 3 };

numbers.Remove(2); // Removes the element 2 from the set

numbers.Remove(4); // Does not remove any element, as 4 is not present in the set

4.4.4 Checking if an Element Exists

To check if an element exists in a set, you can use the Contains method of the HashSet<T> class. The Contains method returns a boolean value indicating whether the element is present in the set. For example:

HashSet<int> numbers = new HashSet<int> { 1, 2, 3 };

bool containsTwo = numbers.Contains(2); // Returns true, as 2 is present in the set

bool containsFour = numbers.Contains(4); // Returns false, as 4 is not present in the set

4.4.5 Set Operations

Sets support various operations such as union, intersection, and difference. These operations allow you to combine or compare sets to produce a new set.

Union

The union of two sets is a set that contains all the elements from both sets, without any duplicates. In C#, you can perform the union operation using the UnionWith method of the HashSet<T> class. The UnionWith method modifies the current set by adding all the elements from another set. For example:

```
HashSet<int> set1 = new HashSet<int> { 1, 2, 3 };
HashSet<int> set2 = new HashSet<int> { 3, 4, 5 };
set1.UnionWith(set2); // Adds the elements 4 and 5 to set1
```

Intersection

The intersection of two sets is a set that contains only the elements that are common to both sets. In C#, you can perform the intersection operation using the IntersectWith method of the HashSet<T> class. The IntersectWith method modifies the current set by removing all the elements that are not present in another set. For example:

```
HashSet<int> set1 = new HashSet<int> { 1, 2, 3 };
HashSet<int> set2 = new HashSet<int> { 3, 4, 5 };
set1.IntersectWith(set2); // Removes the element 1 and 2 from set1
```

Difference

The difference of two sets is a set that contains the elements from the first set that are not present in the second set. In C#, you can perform the difference operation using the ExceptWith method of the HashSet<T> class. The ExceptWith method modifies the current set by removing all the elements that are also present in another set. For example:

```
HashSet<int> set1 = new HashSet<int> { 1, 2, 3 };
HashSet<int> set2 = new HashSet<int> { 3, 4, 5 };
set1.ExceptWith(set2); // Removes the element 3 from set1
```

4.4.6 Enumerating a Set

To iterate over the elements of a set, you can use a foreach loop. The elements will be returned in an arbitrary order, as sets do not maintain any specific order. For example:

```
HashSet<int> numbers = new HashSet<int> { 1, 2, 3 };
foreach (int number in numbers)
{
Console.WriteLine(number);
}
```

This will output:

```
1
```

4.4.7 Conclusion

Sets are a powerful tool in C# for working with collections of unique elements. The HashSet<T> class provides efficient operations for adding, removing, and checking the existence of elements in a set. Additionally, sets support operations such as union, intersection, and difference, allowing you to combine or compare sets to produce a new set. By understanding how to work with sets, you can write more efficient and concise code when dealing with collections in C#.

5 - Methods and Functions

5.1 Defining and Calling Methods

In C#, a method is a block of code that performs a specific task. It is a reusable piece of code that can be called from other parts of the program. Methods are essential in organizing and structuring code, as they help break down complex tasks into smaller, more manageable pieces.

5.1.1 Method Syntax

To define a method in C#, you need to specify its name, return type (if any), and any parameters it accepts. The syntax for defining a method is as follows:

```
access_modifier return_type MethodName(parameter_list)
{
// Method body
// Code to be executed
// Return statement (if applicable)
}
```

Let's break down the different parts of the method syntax:

- **Access Modifier**: Specifies the accessibility of the method (e.g., public, private, protected).
- **Return Type**: Specifies the type of value the method returns. If the method doesn't return a value, the return type is void.
- **Method Name**: The name of the method, which should be descriptive and follow naming conventions.
- **Parameter List**: The list of input parameters the method accepts, if any. Parameters are optional and can be of any valid data type.

Here's an example of a simple method that takes two integers as parameters and returns their sum:

```
public int AddNumbers(int num1, int num2)
{
int sum = num1 + num2;
return sum;
}
```

In this example, the method is named AddNumbers, and it accepts two integer parameters num1 and num2. It calculates the sum of the two numbers and returns the result as an integer.

5.1.2 Calling Methods

Once a method is defined, you can call it from other parts of your program to execute the code inside the method. To call a method, you need to use its name followed by parentheses. If the method has parameters, you need to provide the appropriate arguments inside the parentheses.

Here's an example of calling the AddNumbers method from earlier:

```
int result = AddNumbers(5, 3);
Console.WriteLine(result); // Output: 8
```

In this example, we call the AddNumbers method with arguments 5 and 3. The method calculates the sum and returns the result, which is then stored in the result variable. Finally, we print the result to the console.

5.1.3 Method Overloading

C# allows you to define multiple methods with the same name but different parameter lists. This is known as method overloading. Overloaded methods provide flexibility and allow you to perform similar operations with different types or numbers of parameters.

To overload a method, you need to define multiple methods with the same name but different parameter lists. The compiler determines which method to call based on the arguments provided during the method call.

Here's an example of method overloading:

```csharp
public int AddNumbers(int num1, int num2)
{
int sum = num1 + num2;
return sum;
}
public double AddNumbers(double num1, double num2)
{
double sum = num1 + num2;
return sum;
}
```

In this example, we have two AddNumbers methods. The first method accepts two integers and returns an integer, while the second method accepts two doubles and returns a double. The compiler will choose the appropriate method based on the argument types.

5.1.4 Passing Parameters

Methods can accept parameters, which allow you to pass values to the method for processing. There are two types of parameters in C#: value parameters and reference parameters.

Value Parameters

By default, parameters in C# are passed by value. This means that a copy of the value is passed to the method, and any changes made to the parameter inside the method do not affect the original value.

Here's an example of a method with a value parameter:

```csharp
public void IncrementNumber(int number)
{
number++;
Console.WriteLine(number); // Output: 6
}
int num = 5;
IncrementNumber(num);
```

Console.WriteLine(num); // Output: 5

In this example, the IncrementNumber method takes an integer parameter number. Inside the method, we increment the value of number by 1. However, the original value of num remains unchanged because the parameter is passed by value.

Reference Parameters

To pass a parameter by reference, you need to use the ref or out keyword. When a parameter is passed by reference, any changes made to the parameter inside the method will affect the original value.

Here's an example of a method with a reference parameter:

```
public void IncrementNumber(ref int number)
{
number++;
Console.WriteLine(number); // Output: 6
}
int num = 5;
IncrementNumber(ref num);
Console.WriteLine(num); // Output: 6
```

In this example, we use the ref keyword to pass the num variable by reference to the IncrementNumber method. Any changes made to the number parameter inside the method will affect the original value of num.

5.1.5 Returning Values

Methods can also return values using the return keyword. The return type of the method should match the type specified in the method signature. If a method doesn't return a value, the return type should be void.

Here's an example of a method that returns a value:

```
public int MultiplyNumbers(int num1, int num2)
{
```

```
int product = num1 * num2;
return product;
}
int result = MultiplyNumbers(5, 3);
Console.WriteLine(result); // Output: 15
```

In this example, the MultiplyNumbers method takes two integer parameters and returns their product. The product is then stored in the result variable and printed to the console.

Returning a value allows you to use the result of a method in other parts of your program, making your code more modular and reusable.

Conclusion

In this section, we learned about defining and calling methods in C#. We explored the syntax for defining methods, including the access modifier, return type, method name, and parameter list. We also discussed method overloading, passing parameters by value and by reference, and returning values from methods. Understanding how to define and call methods is crucial for writing clean, modular, and efficient code in C#.

5.2 Method Overloading

In C#, method overloading is a feature that allows you to define multiple methods with the same name but different parameters. This means that you can have multiple methods with the same name, but each method can accept different types or numbers of parameters. Method overloading provides flexibility and convenience when working with methods, as it allows you to perform similar operations with different types of data.

5.2.1 Introduction to Method Overloading

Method overloading is a form of polymorphism, which is one of the fundamental principles of object-oriented programming. Polymorphism allows you to define multiple methods with the same name but different behaviors. In the case of method overloading, the behavior of the method is determined by the parameters it accepts.

When you overload a method, you create multiple versions of the method that can be called based on the arguments passed to it. The compiler determines which version of the method to call based on the number, types, and order of the arguments.

5.2.2 Overloading Methods with Different Parameter Types

One of the most common use cases for method overloading is when you want to perform the same operation on different types of data. For example, let's say you want to create a method called Add that can add two numbers together. You can overload the Add method to accept different types of parameters, such as integers, floating-point numbers, or even strings.

Here's an example of how you can overload the Add method:

```
public class Calculator
{
public int Add(int a, int b)
{
return a + b;
```

```
}
public double Add(double a, double b)
{
return a + b;
}
public string Add(string a, string b)
{
return a + b;
}
}
```

In the example above, we have defined three versions of the Add method. The first version accepts two integers and returns an integer. The second version accepts two doubles and returns a double. The third version accepts two strings and concatenates them together.

By overloading the Add method, you can now call it with different types of arguments and get the desired result:

```
Calculator calculator = new Calculator();
int sum1 = calculator.Add(5, 10); // returns 15
double sum2 = calculator.Add(3.14, 2.71); // returns 5.85
string sum3 = calculator.Add("Hello", "World"); // returns "HelloWorld"
```

5.2.3 Overloading Methods with Different Number of Parameters

In addition to overloading methods with different parameter types, you can also overload methods with a different number of parameters. This allows you to provide different levels of flexibility when calling a method.

Let's take the Add method example from the previous section and add another version that accepts three integers:

```
public class Calculator
{
public int Add(int a, int b)
```

```
{
return a + b;
}
public double Add(double a, double b)
{
return a + b;
}
public string Add(string a, string b)
{
return a + b;
}
public int Add(int a, int b, int c)
{
return a + b + c;
}
}
```

Now, you can call the Add method with two or three integers:

```
Calculator calculator = new Calculator();
int sum1 = calculator.Add(5, 10); // returns 15
int sum2 = calculator.Add(2, 4, 6); // returns 12
```

By overloading the Add method with a different number of parameters, you can provide more flexibility to the users of your class.

5.2.4 Benefits of Method Overloading

Method overloading offers several benefits in C# programming:

1. **Code Reusability**: By overloading methods, you can reuse the same method name for similar operations, reducing code duplication.
2. **Readability**: Overloaded methods provide a clear and concise way to perform similar operations on different types of data, making your code more readable and maintainable.
3. **Flexibility**: Method overloading allows you to provide different levels of flexibility when calling a method, as you can

choose to pass different types or numbers of parameters.

4. **Ease of Use**: Overloaded methods make it easier for developers to use your class or library, as they can call the same method name with different arguments based on their requirements.

5.2.5 Method Overloading Best Practices

When using method overloading, it's important to follow some best practices to ensure clean and maintainable code:

1. **Avoid Ambiguity**: Make sure that the overloaded methods have different parameter types or numbers to avoid ambiguity. If two methods have the same parameter types and numbers, the compiler will generate an error.

2. **Keep it Simple**: Overloading methods should be used to provide different behaviors for similar operations. Avoid overloading methods with vastly different functionalities, as it can lead to confusion and make your code harder to understand.

3. **Consider Naming Conventions**: When overloading methods, choose meaningful and descriptive names that reflect the purpose of each method. This will make your code more readable and self-explanatory.

4. **Document Your Code**: As with any code, it's important to document your overloaded methods to provide clear instructions on how to use them. Use XML comments or other documentation techniques to explain the purpose and behavior of each overloaded method.

By following these best practices, you can effectively use method overloading to enhance the flexibility and readability of your code.

Conclusion

Method overloading is a powerful feature in C# that allows you to define multiple methods with the same name but different parameters. It provides flexibility and convenience when working with methods, allowing you to perform similar operations on different types or numbers of data. By following best practices and understanding the benefits of method overloading, you can write clean and maintainable code that is easy to use and understand.

5.3 Passing Parameters

In C#, parameters are used to pass values to methods or functions. Parameters allow us to provide input to a method and perform operations on that input. There are different ways to pass parameters in C#, including passing by value, passing by reference, and passing by output.

5.3.1 Passing by Value

When we pass a parameter by value, a copy of the value is created and passed to the method. Any changes made to the parameter within the method will not affect the original value. This is the default way of passing parameters in C#.

Let's take a look at an example:

```
public void Increment(int num)
{
num++;
Console.WriteLine("Inside the method: " + num);
}
int number = 10;
Increment(number);
Console.WriteLine("Outside the method: " + number);
Output:
Inside the method: 11
Outside the method: 10
```

In the above example, we have a method called Increment that takes an integer parameter num. Inside the method, we increment the value of num by 1. However, when we print the value of number outside the method, it remains unchanged. This is because the parameter num is passed by value, and any changes made to it inside the method do not affect the original value.

5.3.2 Passing by Reference

Passing a parameter by reference allows us to modify the original value of the parameter within the method. To pass a parameter by reference, we use the ref keyword before the parameter type.

Let's see an example:

```
public void Increment(ref int num)
{
num++;
Console.WriteLine("Inside the method: " + num);
}
int number = 10;
Increment(ref number);
Console.WriteLine("Outside the method: " + number);
Output:
Inside the method: 11
Outside the method: 11
```

In the above example, we have modified the Increment method to accept the parameter num by reference using the ref keyword. Now, when we pass the number variable to the method using ref, any changes made to num inside the method will also affect the original value of number.

5.3.3 Passing by Output

Passing a parameter by output is similar to passing by reference, but with one key difference. When we pass a parameter by output, we are not required to initialize the parameter before passing it to the method. The method is responsible for assigning a value to the parameter before it returns.

To pass a parameter by output, we use the out keyword before the parameter type.

Let's take a look at an example:

```
public void GetSum(int a, int b, out int sum)
{
sum = a + b;
```

```
}
int result;
GetSum(5, 10, out result);
Console.WriteLine("Sum: " + result);
Output:
Sum: 15
```

In the above example, we have a method called GetSum that takes two integer parameters a and b, and an output parameter sum. Inside the method, we calculate the sum of a and b and assign it to the sum parameter. When we call the method, we pass the result variable as the output parameter. After the method call, the value of result is updated with the sum calculated inside the method.

5.3.4 Default Parameters

C# allows us to define default values for parameters. When a default value is specified for a parameter, it becomes optional, and we can omit it when calling the method. If no value is provided for an optional parameter, the default value is used.

Let's see an example:

```
public void Greet(string name, string message = "Hello")
{
Console.WriteLine(message + ", " + name + "!");
}
Greet("John");
Greet("Emily", "Hi");
Output:
Hello, John!
Hi, Emily!
```

In the above example, we have a method called Greet that takes two string parameters name and message. The message parameter has a default value of "Hello". When we call the method without providing a value for message, the default value is used. However, if we provide a value for message, it overrides the default value.

5.3.5 Params Parameters

C# provides the params keyword to allow a variable number of arguments to be passed to a method. The params parameter must be an array, and we can pass any number of arguments of the specified type.

Let's take a look at an example:

```
public void PrintNumbers(params int[] numbers)
{
foreach (int number in numbers)
{
Console.WriteLine(number);
}
}
PrintNumbers(1, 2, 3);
PrintNumbers(4, 5, 6, 7);
Output:
1
2
3
4
5
6
7
```

In the above example, we have a method called PrintNumbers that takes a params parameter of type int[]. We can pass any number of integer arguments to this method, and they will be treated as an array inside the method. We can then iterate over the array and print each number.

Conclusion

Passing parameters is an essential concept in C# programming. By understanding the different ways to pass parameters, such as passing by value, passing by reference, and passing by output, we can effectively utilize methods and functions to perform operations on input values.

Additionally, default parameters and params parameters provide flexibility and convenience when working with methods that require optional or variable numbers of arguments.

5.4 Returning Values

In C#, a method can return a value to the caller. This allows the method to perform some computation or manipulation and provide the result back to the calling code. Returning values from methods is an essential concept in programming, as it enables the reuse of code and facilitates the flow of data between different parts of a program.

5.4.1 Returning a Single Value

To return a single value from a method, you need to specify the return type in the method signature. The return type indicates the type of value that the method will return. For example, if you want to create a method that calculates the sum of two numbers and returns the result, you can define the method like this:

```
public int CalculateSum(int num1, int num2)
{
int sum = num1 + num2;
return sum;
}
```

In this example, the method CalculateSum takes two integer parameters num1 and num2 and calculates their sum. The int return type indicates that the method will return an integer value. The return keyword is used to return the computed sum back to the caller.

To use the returned value, you can assign it to a variable or use it directly in an expression. For example:

```
int result = CalculateSum(5, 3);
Console.WriteLine("The sum is: " + result);
```

In this code snippet, the CalculateSum method is called with the arguments 5 and 3. The returned value, which is the sum of the two numbers, is assigned to the variable result and then printed to the console.

5.4.2 Returning Multiple Values

In some cases, you may need to return multiple values from a method. C# provides several ways to achieve this, such as using tuples, out parameters, or custom data structures.

5.4.2.1 Tuples

Tuples are a convenient way to return multiple values from a method. A tuple is an ordered collection of elements, each of which can have a different type. To return multiple values using tuples, you can define the return type of the method as a tuple. For example:

```csharp
public (int, int) GetMinMax(int[] numbers)
{
int min = numbers[0];
int max = numbers[0];
for (int i = 1; i < numbers.Length; i++)
{
if (numbers[i] < min)
min = numbers[i];
if (numbers[i] > max)
max = numbers[i];
}
return (min, max);
}
```

In this example, the method GetMinMax takes an array of integers as a parameter and finds the minimum and maximum values in the array. The return type of the method is (int, int), indicating that it will return a tuple with two integer values.

To use the returned values, you can destructure the tuple into separate variables or access its elements directly. For example:

```csharp
int[] numbers = { 5, 2, 9, 1, 7 };
var (min, max) = GetMinMax(numbers);
Console.WriteLine("Minimum: " + min);
```

Console.WriteLine("Maximum: " + max);

In this code snippet, the GetMinMax method is called with the numbers array. The returned tuple is deconstructed into the variables min and max, which are then printed to the console.

5.4.2.2 Out Parameters

Another way to return multiple values from a method is by using out parameters. An out parameter is a parameter that is used to return a value from a method. To define an out parameter, you need to use the out keyword in the method signature. For example:

```
public void GetMinMax(int[] numbers, out int min, out int max)
{
min = numbers[0];
max = numbers[0];
for (int i = 1; i < numbers.Length; i++)
{
if (numbers[i] < min)
min = numbers[i];
if (numbers[i] > max)
max = numbers[i];
}
}
```

In this example, the method GetMinMax takes an array of integers as a parameter and finds the minimum and maximum values in the array. The min and max parameters are defined as out parameters, indicating that they will be used to return the computed values.

To use the returned values, you need to declare the out parameters before calling the method. For example:

```
int[] numbers = { 5, 2, 9, 1, 7 };
int min, max;
GetMinMax(numbers, out min, out max);
```

```
Console.WriteLine("Minimum: " + min);
Console.WriteLine("Maximum: " + max);
```

In this code snippet, the GetMinMax method is called with the numbers array and the min and max variables as out parameters. The computed minimum and maximum values are then printed to the console.

5.4.2.3 Custom Data Structures

If you need to return multiple values of different types or want more control over the returned data, you can create a custom data structure to hold the values. This can be done by defining a class or a struct with properties or fields to store the values. For example:

```csharp
public class Person
{
public string Name { get; set; }
public int Age { get; set; }
}
public Person GetPerson()
{
Person person = new Person();
person.Name = "John";
person.Age = 30;
return person;
}
```

In this example, the GetPerson method creates a new instance of the Person class, sets its properties, and returns it to the caller.

To use the returned values, you can assign them to variables and access their properties. For example:

```csharp
Person person = GetPerson();
Console.WriteLine("Name: " + person.Name);
Console.WriteLine("Age: " + person.Age);
```

In this code snippet, the GetPerson method is called, and the returned Person object is assigned to the person variable. The properties of the person object are then printed to the console.

5.4.3 Returning from Constructors

Constructors are special methods used to initialize objects of a class. In C#, constructors do not have a return type, as their purpose is to create and initialize an object. However, you can indirectly return a value from a constructor by using the out keyword in the constructor signature. This allows you to initialize an object and return it to the caller. For example:

```
public class Person
{
public string Name { get; set; }
public int Age { get; set; }
public Person(string name, int age, out bool isValid)
{
isValid = !string.IsNullOrEmpty(name) && age > 0;
if (isValid)
{
Name = name;
Age = age;
}
}
}
```

In this example, the Person class has a constructor that takes a name and age parameter. The constructor also has an out parameter isValid, which is used to indicate whether the object was successfully initialized.

To use the returned object, you need to declare the isValid parameter before creating an instance of the Person class. For example:

```
bool isValid;
Person person = new Person("John", 30, out isValid);
```

```
if (isValid)
{
Console.WriteLine("Name: " + person.Name);
Console.WriteLine("Age: " + person.Age);
}
else
{
Console.WriteLine("Invalid person data.");
}
```

In this code snippet, the Person constructor is called with the name, age, and isValid parameters. The isValid parameter is used to check if the object was successfully initialized. If it is valid, the properties of the person object are printed to the console. Otherwise, an error message is displayed.

Returning values from methods is a powerful feature in C# that allows you to create reusable and modular code. By returning values, you can pass data between different parts of your program and perform complex computations. Whether you need to return a single value or multiple values, C# provides various mechanisms to accomplish this task.

6 - Object-Oriented Programming

6.1 Classes and Objects

In object-oriented programming, classes and objects are fundamental concepts. They allow us to create reusable code and model real-world entities in our programs. In this section, we will explore the concepts of classes and objects in C#.

6.1.1 Introduction to Classes

A class is a blueprint or template for creating objects. It defines the properties and behaviors that an object of that class will have. In other words, a class is a user-defined data type that encapsulates data and methods.

To define a class in C#, we use the class keyword followed by the class name. Here's an example of a simple class called Person:

```
public class Person
{
// Properties
public string Name { get; set; }
public int Age { get; set; }
// Methods
public void SayHello()
{
Console.WriteLine("Hello, my name is " + Name);
}
}
```

In the above example, the Person class has two properties: Name and Age. These properties define the state of a person object. The SayHello method is a behavior of the Person class, which allows a person object to introduce themselves.

6.1.2 Creating Objects

Once we have defined a class, we can create objects of that class. An object is an instance of a class. It represents a specific entity based on the class blueprint.

To create an object in C#, we use the new keyword followed by the class name and parentheses. Here's an example of creating two Person objects:

Person person1 = new Person();

person1.Name = "John";

person1.Age = 25;

Person person2 = new Person();

person2.Name = "Jane";

person2.Age = 30;

In the above example, we create two Person objects: person1 and person2. We then set the Name and Age properties of each object.

6.1.3 Accessing Object Members

Once we have created an object, we can access its members (properties and methods) using the dot notation. The dot notation allows us to access the members of an object.

Console.WriteLine(person1.Name); // Output: John

person1.SayHello(); // Output: Hello, my name is John

In the above example, we access the Name property of person1 and call the SayHello method on person1.

6.1.4 Constructors

A constructor is a special method that is called when an object of a class is created. It is used to initialize the object's state. In C#, a constructor has the same name as the class and does not have a return type.

public class Person

{

public string Name { get; set; }

public int Age { get; set; }

// Default constructor

public Person()

{

Name = "Unknown";

```
Age = 0;
}
// Parameterized constructor
public Person(string name, int age)
{
Name = name;
Age = age;
}
public void SayHello()
{
Console.WriteLine("Hello, my name is " + Name);
}
}
```

In the above example, we have defined two constructors for the Person class. The default constructor initializes the Name and Age properties with default values. The parameterized constructor allows us to initialize the Name and Age properties with custom values.

6.1.5 Static Members

In addition to instance members (properties and methods), a class can also have static members. Static members belong to the class itself, rather than to any specific object of the class. They are shared among all objects of the class.

```
public class MathUtils
{
public static int Add(int a, int b)
{
return a + b;
}
}
```

In the above example, the Add method of the MathUtils class is a static method. We can call this method without creating an object of the class.

```
int result = MathUtils.Add(5, 3);
Console.WriteLine(result); // Output: 8
```

6.1.6 Encapsulation

Encapsulation is one of the core principles of object-oriented programming. It refers to the bundling of data and methods within a class, and controlling access to that data and methods.

In C#, we can achieve encapsulation by using access modifiers. There are four access modifiers in C#: public, private, protected, and internal. These modifiers control the visibility and accessibility of class members.

- public: The member is accessible from any code.
- private: The member is only accessible from within the class.
- protected: The member is accessible from within the class and its derived classes.
- internal: The member is accessible from within the same assembly.

By default, class members are private if no access modifier is specified.

```
public class Person
{
private string name;
private int age;
public string Name
{
get { return name; }
set { name = value; }
}
public int Age
{
get { return age; }
set { age = value; }
```

```
}
public void SayHello()
{
Console.WriteLine("Hello, my name is " + Name);
}
}
```

In the above example, the name and age fields are private, which means they can only be accessed within the Person class. The Name and Age properties provide controlled access to these fields.

6.1.7 Summary

In this section, we learned about classes and objects in C#. We explored how to define a class, create objects, access object members, use constructors, work with static members, and achieve encapsulation. Understanding these concepts is crucial for mastering C# and building robust and maintainable applications.

6.2 Inheritance

Inheritance is a fundamental concept in object-oriented programming (OOP) that allows you to create new classes based on existing classes. It is a mechanism that enables code reuse and promotes the concept of "is-a" relationship between classes. In C#, inheritance is achieved using the : symbol followed by the name of the base class.

6.2.1 Base and Derived Classes

Inheritance involves two types of classes: base classes and derived classes. A base class is the class from which other classes inherit properties and methods. It serves as a blueprint for the derived classes. On the other hand, a derived class is a class that inherits properties and methods from a base class.

To create a derived class, you specify the base class after the : symbol in the class declaration. The derived class inherits all the members (fields, properties, and methods) of the base class, except for constructors and destructors. This means that you can access and use the members of the base class in the derived class.

```
class BaseClass
{
// Base class members
}
class DerivedClass : BaseClass
{
// Derived class members
}
```

6.2.2 Access Modifiers and Inheritance

When working with inheritance, access modifiers play an important role in determining the visibility and accessibility of members in the derived class. In C#, there are four access modifiers: public, private, protected, and internal.

- public: The member is accessible from any code within the same assembly or from any derived class.
- private: The member is only accessible within the same class and cannot be accessed from derived classes.
- protected: The member is accessible within the same class and derived classes, but not from other classes.
- internal: The member is accessible within the same assembly but not from outside the assembly.

By default, if no access modifier is specified, members are considered private within a class and internal outside the class.

6.2.3 Method Overriding

One of the key features of inheritance is the ability to override methods defined in the base class. Method overriding allows you to provide a different implementation of a method in the derived class. To override a method, you use the override keyword in the derived class.

```
class BaseClass
{
public virtual void Print()
{
Console.WriteLine("Base class method");
}
}
class DerivedClass : BaseClass
{
public override void Print()
{
Console.WriteLine("Derived class method");
}
}
```

In the example above, the Print method in the derived class overrides the implementation of the Print method in the base class.

When you call the Print method on an instance of the derived class, it will execute the overridden method instead of the base class method.

6.2.4 Base Keyword

The base keyword in C# is used to access members of the base class from within the derived class. It is particularly useful when you want to call the base class constructor or access base class members that have been overridden in the derived class.

To call the base class constructor, you use the base keyword followed by the constructor arguments. This allows you to initialize the base class before initializing the derived class.

```
class BaseClass
{
public BaseClass(string message)
{
Console.WriteLine(message);
}
}
class DerivedClass : BaseClass
{
public DerivedClass() : base("Calling base class constructor")
{
// Derived class constructor
}
}
```

In the example above, the derived class constructor calls the base class constructor using the base keyword and passes a message as an argument. This ensures that the base class is properly initialized before the derived class.

6.2.5 Multiple Inheritance

C# does not support multiple inheritance, which means that a class cannot inherit from multiple base classes. This design decision was made to avoid the complexities and ambiguities that can arise from multiple inheritance.

However, C# provides an alternative to multiple inheritance through interfaces. An interface defines a contract that a class must implement, and a class can implement multiple interfaces. This allows you to achieve similar functionality to multiple inheritance by defining common behavior in interfaces and implementing them in different classes.

```csharp
interface IShape
{
void Draw();
}
class Circle : IShape
{
public void Draw()
{
Console.WriteLine("Drawing a circle");
}
}
class Rectangle : IShape
{
public void Draw()
{
Console.WriteLine("Drawing a rectangle");
}
}
```

In the example above, the Circle and Rectangle classes implement the IShape interface, which defines a Draw method. This allows both classes to have their own implementation of the Draw method while sharing a common interface.

6.2.6 Abstract Classes

An abstract class is a class that cannot be instantiated and is meant to be inherited by other classes. It serves as a base class for other classes and provides a common interface or behavior that derived classes must implement.

To define an abstract class, you use the abstract keyword in the class declaration. An abstract class can have abstract members (methods, properties, and events) that do not have an implementation. These abstract members must be implemented in the derived classes.

```
abstract class Shape
{
public abstract void Draw();
}
class Circle : Shape
{
public override void Draw()
{
Console.WriteLine("Drawing a circle");
}
}
class Rectangle : Shape
{
public override void Draw()
{
Console.WriteLine("Drawing a rectangle");
}
}
```

In the example above, the Shape class is an abstract class that defines an abstract Draw method. The Circle and Rectangle classes inherit from the Shape class and provide their own implementation of the Draw method.

Abstract classes are useful when you want to define a common interface or behavior for a group of related classes, but you do not want to instantiate the abstract class itself.

Conclusion

Inheritance is a powerful feature of C# that allows you to create new classes based on existing classes. It promotes code reuse and enables you to model real-world relationships between objects. By understanding inheritance and its related concepts, you can design and implement more flexible and maintainable software systems.

6.3 Polymorphism

Polymorphism is a fundamental concept in object-oriented programming that allows objects of different classes to be treated as objects of a common base class. It enables us to write code that can work with objects of different types, providing flexibility and extensibility to our programs.

6.3.1 Understanding Polymorphism

Polymorphism is derived from the Greek words "poly" meaning many and "morph" meaning form. In the context of object-oriented programming, polymorphism refers to the ability of an object to take on many forms. It allows us to write code that can operate on objects of different classes, as long as they share a common base class or interface.

At its core, polymorphism allows us to write code that is more generic and reusable. Instead of writing separate code for each specific class, we can write code that works with a common base class or interface, and it will automatically work with any derived classes that inherit from it.

6.3.2 Polymorphism in Action

To understand how polymorphism works, let's consider an example. Suppose we have a base class called Shape and two derived classes called Circle and Rectangle. Both Circle and Rectangle inherit from the Shape class.

```
public class Shape
{
public virtual void Draw()
{
Console.WriteLine("Drawing a shape");
}
}
public class Circle : Shape
{
```

```csharp
public override void Draw()
{
Console.WriteLine("Drawing a circle");
}
}
public class Rectangle : Shape
{
public override void Draw()
{
Console.WriteLine("Drawing a rectangle");
}
}
```

In the above example, the Shape class has a virtual method called Draw(), which is overridden in the derived classes Circle and Rectangle. Each derived class provides its own implementation of the Draw() method.

Now, let's see how polymorphism allows us to work with objects of different types using a common base class:

```csharp
Shape shape1 = new Circle();
Shape shape2 = new Rectangle();
shape1.Draw(); // Output: Drawing a circle
shape2.Draw(); // Output: Drawing a rectangle
```

In the above code, we create two variables shape1 and shape2 of type Shape, but we assign objects of type Circle and Rectangle to them, respectively. When we call the Draw() method on these objects, the appropriate implementation of the method is executed based on the actual type of the object.

This is the power of polymorphism. We can write code that works with objects of different types, without having to know the specific type at compile-time. This allows us to write more flexible and extensible code.

6.3.3 Polymorphism and Method Overriding

Polymorphism is closely related to method overriding. When a derived class overrides a method of its base class, it provides its own implementation of the method. This allows us to call the overridden method on objects of the derived class, even if they are stored in variables of the base class type.

In the previous example, the Draw() method is overridden in the Circle and Rectangle classes. When we call the Draw() method on objects of these classes, the overridden implementation is executed.

```
Circle circle = new Circle();
Rectangle rectangle = new Rectangle();
circle.Draw(); // Output: Drawing a circle
rectangle.Draw(); // Output: Drawing a rectangle
```

In the above code, we create objects of type Circle and Rectangle and call the Draw() method on them. Since the Draw() method is overridden in both classes, the respective implementations are executed.

6.3.4 Polymorphism and Abstract Classes

Polymorphism can also be achieved using abstract classes. An abstract class is a class that cannot be instantiated and is meant to be inherited by other classes. It can contain abstract methods, which are meant to be overridden by the derived classes.

```
public abstract class Shape
{
public abstract void Draw();
}
public class Circle : Shape
{
public override void Draw()
{
Console.WriteLine("Drawing a circle");
}
}
```

```
public class Rectangle : Shape
{
public override void Draw()
{
Console.WriteLine("Drawing a rectangle");
}
}
```

In the above example, the Shape class is declared as abstract, and it contains an abstract method called Draw(). The derived classes Circle and Rectangle override the Draw() method and provide their own implementations.

Now, let's see how polymorphism works with abstract classes:

```
Shape shape1 = new Circle();
Shape shape2 = new Rectangle();
shape1.Draw(); // Output: Drawing a circle
shape2.Draw(); // Output: Drawing a rectangle
```

In the above code, we create variables of type Shape and assign objects of type Circle and Rectangle to them. When we call the Draw() method on these objects, the overridden implementations in the derived classes are executed.

6.3.5 Benefits of Polymorphism

Polymorphism offers several benefits in object-oriented programming:

1. Code Reusability: Polymorphism allows us to write code that can work with objects of different types, reducing code duplication and improving code reusability.

2. Flexibility: Polymorphism provides flexibility by allowing us to write code that can operate on objects of different classes, as long as they share a common base class or interface. This makes our code more adaptable to changes and easier to maintain.

3. Extensibility: Polymorphism allows us to easily extend our

code by adding new derived classes that inherit from a common base class. This makes it easier to add new functionality to our programs without modifying existing code.

4. Simplified Code: Polymorphism simplifies code by allowing us to write more generic code that can handle a wide range of objects. This reduces the complexity of our code and makes it easier to understand and maintain.

In conclusion, polymorphism is a powerful concept in object-oriented programming that allows objects of different classes to be treated as objects of a common base class. It provides flexibility, extensibility, and code reusability, making our code more efficient and maintainable. By understanding and utilizing polymorphism effectively, we can write more robust and flexible programs in C#.

6.4 Encapsulation

Encapsulation is one of the fundamental principles of object-oriented programming (OOP) and plays a crucial role in C#. It is the process of hiding the internal details of an object and providing a public interface to interact with it. Encapsulation allows us to control access to the internal state and behavior of an object, ensuring that it is used correctly and preventing unauthorized modifications.

6.4.1 What is Encapsulation?

Encapsulation combines data and methods into a single unit called a class. The class encapsulates the data by declaring it as private, which means it can only be accessed within the class itself. The methods, on the other hand, are declared as public, allowing them to be accessed from outside the class.

By encapsulating the data, we can ensure that it is accessed and modified only through the defined methods. This provides a level of abstraction, allowing us to change the internal implementation of the class without affecting the code that uses it. It also helps in maintaining the integrity of the data by enforcing validation rules and business logic.

6.4.2 Access Modifiers

C# provides different access modifiers that control the visibility and accessibility of members (fields, properties, and methods) within a class. These access modifiers are used to implement encapsulation and define the level of access to the members.

The following are the access modifiers available in C#:

- **public**: The member is accessible from any code within the same assembly or from any other assembly.
- **private**: The member is accessible only from within the same class.

- **protected**: The member is accessible within the same class and its derived classes.
- **internal**: The member is accessible from any code within the same assembly but not from other assemblies.
- **protected internal**: The member is accessible within the same assembly and its derived classes, even if they are in different assemblies.

By using these access modifiers appropriately, we can control the visibility of the members and ensure that they are accessed only as intended.

6.4.3 Benefits of Encapsulation

Encapsulation offers several benefits in software development:

1. **Data Hiding**: Encapsulation hides the internal details of an object, preventing direct access to its data. This protects the data from being modified accidentally or maliciously, ensuring data integrity.
2. **Code Reusability**: By encapsulating data and behavior into classes, we can reuse the code in different parts of the application. This promotes code modularity and reduces code duplication.
3. **Abstraction**: Encapsulation provides a level of abstraction by exposing only the necessary information through the public interface. This simplifies the usage of the class and hides the complexity of its implementation.
4. **Security**: Encapsulation helps in securing sensitive data by controlling access to it. By making the data private and providing controlled access through methods, we can enforce security measures and prevent unauthorized access.
5. **Maintenance and Flexibility**: Encapsulation allows us to change the internal implementation of a class without

affecting the code that uses it. This provides flexibility in making modifications and simplifies maintenance.

6. **Code Organization**: Encapsulation promotes code organization by grouping related data and behavior into classes. This improves code readability and maintainability.

6.4.4 Guidelines for Encapsulation

To effectively use encapsulation in C#, consider the following guidelines:

1. **Keep data private**: Encapsulate data by declaring it as private and provide public methods to access and modify it. This ensures that the data is accessed and modified only through the defined methods, allowing better control and validation.

2. **Use properties**: Properties provide a controlled way to access and modify the data of an object. They allow us to define custom logic for getting and setting values, enabling validation and additional functionality.

3. **Avoid exposing internal implementation**: The public interface of a class should provide the necessary functionality without exposing the internal implementation details. This allows us to change the implementation without affecting the code that uses the class.

4. **Follow naming conventions**: Use meaningful and descriptive names for classes, methods, and variables. This improves code readability and makes it easier to understand the purpose and functionality of the encapsulated elements.

5. **Consider immutability**: In some cases, it may be beneficial to make objects immutable, meaning their state cannot be changed once created. This ensures that the object remains in a consistent state and simplifies concurrency and thread safety.

6. **Document the public interface**: Provide clear and concise documentation for the public methods and properties of a

class. This helps other developers understand how to use the class correctly and what to expect from its behavior.

By following these guidelines, you can effectively apply encapsulation in your C# code and reap the benefits it offers.

Conclusion

Encapsulation is a fundamental principle of object-oriented programming that promotes code organization, security, and maintainability. By encapsulating data and behavior into classes, we can control access to the internal state of an object and provide a public interface for interaction. This ensures that the object is used correctly and prevents unauthorized modifications. By following the guidelines for encapsulation, you can write clean and maintainable code in C#.

7 - Exception Handling

7.1 Understanding Exceptions

In any programming language, errors and exceptions are inevitable. They can occur due to various reasons such as incorrect input, hardware failures, or unexpected conditions. As a C# developer, it is crucial to understand how to handle these exceptions effectively to ensure the stability and reliability of your applications.

7.1.1 What are Exceptions?

An exception is an abnormal condition or event that occurs during the execution of a program, which disrupts the normal flow of the program's instructions. When an exception occurs, the program's execution is immediately halted, and the runtime environment looks for an exception handler to handle the exception.

In C#, exceptions are represented by objects derived from the System.Exception class. These exception objects contain information about the type of exception, the location where the exception occurred, and any additional data related to the exception.

7.1.2 Types of Exceptions

C# provides a wide range of exception types that cover various error scenarios. Some of the commonly used exception types include:

- System.NullReferenceException: This exception occurs when you try to access a member or invoke a method on a null reference.
- System.IndexOutOfRangeException: This exception occurs when you try to access an array or collection with an index that is outside the valid range.
- System.DivideByZeroException: This exception occurs when you attempt to divide an integer or decimal number by zero.
- System.InvalidCastException: This exception occurs when an invalid type conversion is attempted.
- System.IO.IOException: This exception occurs when an

input/output operation fails, such as reading from or writing to a file.

These are just a few examples of the many exception types available in C#. Each exception type is designed to handle specific error conditions, allowing you to handle exceptions more precisely.

7.1.3 The Exception Hierarchy

In C#, exceptions are organized in a hierarchical structure. At the root of the hierarchy is the System.Exception class, which serves as the base class for all exceptions in C#. This allows you to catch and handle exceptions at a higher level, providing a more general error handling mechanism.

The System.Exception class has several derived classes, such as System.SystemException and System.ApplicationException. The System.SystemException class represents exceptions that are thrown by the runtime environment or the .NET Framework, while the System.ApplicationException class is intended to be used as a base class for custom exceptions.

By understanding the exception hierarchy, you can catch and handle exceptions at different levels of granularity. This allows you to handle specific exceptions separately from more general exceptions, providing a more robust error handling mechanism.

7.1.4 The Try-Catch-Finally Block

In C#, exceptions are typically handled using the try-catch-finally block. The try block contains the code that may throw an exception, while the catch block is used to catch and handle the exception. The finally block is optional and is used to specify code that should be executed regardless of whether an exception occurs or not.

Here is the basic syntax of the try-catch-finally block:

```
try
{
// Code that may throw an exception
}
```

```
catch (ExceptionType1 ex)
{
// Handle ExceptionType1
}
catch (ExceptionType2 ex)
{
// Handle ExceptionType2
}
finally
{
// Code that should be executed regardless of whether an
exception occurs or not
}
```

In the catch block, you specify the type of exception you want to catch. If an exception of that type or any of its derived types is thrown, the corresponding catch block is executed. You can have multiple catch blocks to handle different types of exceptions.

The finally block is optional and is used to specify code that should be executed regardless of whether an exception occurs or not. This block is commonly used to release resources or perform cleanup operations.

7.1.5 Throwing Exceptions

In addition to handling exceptions, you can also explicitly throw exceptions in your code. This can be useful when you want to indicate that a certain condition or error has occurred.

To throw an exception, you use the throw keyword followed by an instance of an exception class. For example:

```
if (age < 0)
{
throw new ArgumentException("Age cannot be negative.");
}
```

In this example, if the age variable is less than zero, an ArgumentException is thrown with the specified error message. This allows you to communicate the error condition to the caller of the method or to the higher-level exception handler.

7.1.6 Custom Exceptions

While C# provides a wide range of built-in exception types, there may be situations where you need to define your own custom exception types. Custom exceptions can be useful when you want to provide more specific information about the error condition or when you want to add additional properties or methods to the exception class.

To define a custom exception, you create a new class that derives from the System.Exception class or one of its derived classes. You can then add any additional properties or methods that are relevant to your exception.

Here is an example of a custom exception class:

```
public class CustomException : Exception
{
public CustomException(string message) : base(message)
{
// Additional initialization code
}
// Additional properties and methods
}
```

In this example, the CustomException class derives from the System.Exception class and adds a constructor that accepts a message parameter. This allows you to provide a custom error message when throwing the exception.

By creating custom exceptions, you can provide more meaningful error messages and handle specific error conditions more effectively.

Conclusion

Understanding exceptions and how to handle them is essential for writing robust and reliable C# applications. By using the try-catch-finally block and throwing exceptions when necessary, you can effectively handle errors and ensure the stability of your code. Additionally, by creating custom exceptions, you can provide more specific information about error conditions and enhance the error handling capabilities of your applications.

7.2 Try-Catch-Finally

Exception handling is an essential aspect of any programming language, including C#. It allows you to gracefully handle errors and exceptions that may occur during the execution of your code. In C#, the try-catch-finally block is used to implement exception handling.

7.2.1 The Try Block

The try block is where you place the code that might throw an exception. It is enclosed within the try keyword followed by an opening and closing curly brace. Any code within the try block is monitored for exceptions. If an exception occurs, the execution of the try block is immediately halted, and the control is transferred to the catch block.

Here's an example of a try block:

```
try
{
// Code that might throw an exception
}
```

7.2.2 The Catch Block

The catch block is used to catch and handle exceptions that occur within the try block. It is preceded by the catch keyword followed by an opening and closing curly brace. Inside the catch block, you can specify the type of exception you want to catch using the exception type as a parameter.

Here's an example of a catch block:

```
try
{
// Code that might throw an exception
}
catch (ExceptionType ex)
{
// Code to handle the exception
}
```

In the above example, ExceptionType represents the type of exception you want to catch. It can be any exception type, such as DivideByZeroException, FileNotFoundException, or InvalidOperationException. If an exception of the specified type occurs in the try block, the catch block is executed.

7.2.3 The Finally Block

The finally block is optional and is used to specify code that should always be executed, regardless of whether an exception occurs or not. It is preceded by the finally keyword followed by an opening and closing curly brace. The code inside the finally block is executed after the try block and catch block, regardless of whether an exception occurred or not.

Here's an example of a finally block:

```
try
{
// Code that might throw an exception
}
catch (ExceptionType ex)
{
// Code to handle the exception
}
finally
{
// Code that always executes
}
```

In the above example, the code inside the finally block will always execute, regardless of whether an exception occurred or not. This is useful for releasing resources, closing connections, or performing any necessary cleanup operations.

7.2.4 Multiple Catch Blocks

You can have multiple catch blocks following a single try block. Each catch block can handle a different type of exception. This allows you to handle different exceptions in different ways.

Here's an example of multiple catch blocks:

```
try
{
// Code that might throw an exception
}
catch (ExceptionType1 ex)
{
// Code to handle ExceptionType1
}
catch (ExceptionType2 ex)
{
// Code to handle ExceptionType2
}
```

In the above example, if an exception of ExceptionType1 occurs, the first catch block will be executed. If an exception of ExceptionType2 occurs, the second catch block will be executed. If none of the specified exceptions occur, the catch blocks will be skipped, and the program will continue executing after the try-catch-finally block.

7.2.5 Rethrowing Exceptions

Sometimes, you may want to catch an exception, perform some additional operations, and then rethrow the exception to be caught by an outer catch block. This can be achieved using the throw statement without any arguments.

Here's an example of rethrowing an exception:

```
try
{
// Code that might throw an exception
}
```

```
catch (ExceptionType ex)
{
// Code to handle the exception
throw;
}
```

In the above example, the catch block catches the exception, performs some operations, and then rethrows the exception using the throw statement. The rethrown exception can then be caught by an outer catch block or handled by the runtime environment.

7.2.6 Nested Try-Catch-Finally Blocks

You can nest try-catch-finally blocks within each other to handle exceptions at different levels of your code. This allows you to handle exceptions at a more granular level and provide specific error handling for different parts of your code.

Here's an example of nested try-catch-finally blocks:

```
try
{
// Outer try block
try
{
// Inner try block
}
catch (ExceptionType1 ex)
{
// Code to handle ExceptionType1 in the inner catch block
}
finally
{
// Code in the inner finally block
}
}
catch (ExceptionType2 ex)
```

```
{
// Code to handle ExceptionType2 in the outer catch block
}
finally
{
// Code in the outer finally block
}
```

In the above example, the outer try block contains an inner try block. If an exception of ExceptionType1 occurs in the inner try block, the inner catch block will handle it. If an exception of ExceptionType2 occurs in the outer try block or the inner try block, the outer catch block will handle it. The finally blocks are executed in the reverse order of their declaration, meaning the inner finally block executes before the outer finally block.

7.2.7 Exception Propagation

When an exception occurs and is not caught within a method, it is propagated up the call stack until it is caught or the program terminates. This allows exceptions to be handled at higher levels of the code hierarchy.

By using try-catch-finally blocks, you can catch exceptions at the appropriate level and handle them accordingly. This prevents the program from crashing and provides a way to gracefully recover from errors.

Conclusion

The try-catch-finally block is a powerful mechanism for handling exceptions in C#. It allows you to write code that can gracefully handle errors and exceptions, ensuring the stability and reliability of your applications. By understanding how to use try-catch-finally blocks effectively, you can enhance the robustness of your code and provide a better user experience.

7.3 Throwing Exceptions

In the previous section, we discussed how to handle exceptions using the try-catch-finally block. However, there are situations where you may want to explicitly throw an exception to indicate that something unexpected or erroneous has occurred in your code. In this section, we will explore how to throw exceptions in C#.

7.3.1 The throw Statement

In C#, the throw statement is used to explicitly throw an exception. It allows you to create and throw an instance of any exception class. The general syntax of the throw statement is as follows:

throw new ExceptionType("Exception message");

Here, ExceptionType is the type of exception you want to throw, and "Exception message" is an optional message that provides additional information about the exception. The exception message is typically used to describe the cause or nature of the exception.

Let's consider an example where we want to throw an exception if a user tries to withdraw more money from their bank account than they have available:

```
public void Withdraw(decimal amount)
{
if (amount > Balance)
{
throw new InvalidOperationException("Insufficient funds");
}
// Perform the withdrawal
Balance -= amount;
}
```

In this example, if the amount parameter is greater than the current balance, we throw an InvalidOperationException with the message "Insufficient funds". This indicates to the caller that the withdrawal cannot be completed due to insufficient funds.

7.3.2 Throwing Built-in Exceptions

C# provides a wide range of built-in exception classes that you can use to handle different types of errors. Some commonly used built-in exception classes include ArgumentException, ArgumentNullException, InvalidOperationException, and NotSupportedException, among others.

When throwing a built-in exception, you can provide additional information by passing a message to the exception constructor. For example:

throw new ArgumentException("Invalid argument value");

In this case, we are throwing an ArgumentException with the message "Invalid argument value". This can be useful when validating method arguments or input parameters.

7.3.3 Creating Custom Exceptions

In addition to using built-in exception classes, you can also create your own custom exception classes to handle specific types of errors in your application. Custom exceptions can provide more specific information about the error and can be used to differentiate between different types of exceptions.

To create a custom exception, you need to define a new class that derives from the Exception base class or one of its derived classes. Here's an example of a custom exception class:

```
public class CustomException : Exception
{
public CustomException(string message) : base(message)
{
}
}
```

In this example, we define a custom exception class called CustomException that inherits from the Exception class. We provide a constructor that takes a message parameter and passes it to the base Exception class constructor.

Once you have defined your custom exception class, you can throw instances of it using the throw statement, just like any other exception. For example:

throw new CustomException("Custom exception message");

7.3.4 Exception Propagation

When an exception is thrown, it can be caught and handled at different levels of the call stack. If an exception is not caught and handled within a method, it will propagate up the call stack until it is caught by an appropriate catch block or until it reaches the top-level of the application, where it may cause the application to terminate.

Exception propagation allows you to handle exceptions at the appropriate level of your code. For example, if a method encounters an exception that it cannot handle, it can throw the exception to its caller, which may have more context or knowledge about how to handle the exception.

7.3.5 Best Practices for Throwing Exceptions

When throwing exceptions in your code, it is important to follow some best practices to ensure that your exceptions are meaningful and helpful for debugging and troubleshooting. Here are some guidelines to consider:

- Throw exceptions for exceptional conditions: Only throw exceptions for situations that are truly exceptional and unexpected. Avoid using exceptions for normal flow control or error handling.
- Provide meaningful exception messages: When throwing exceptions, provide clear and concise messages that describe the cause or nature of the exception. This will help developers understand the error and troubleshoot the issue more effectively.
- Use appropriate exception types: Choose the most appropriate built-in exception class or create custom exception classes that accurately represent the type of error

being encountered. This will make it easier to handle and differentiate between different types of exceptions.

- Include relevant information in exceptions: If possible, include additional information in the exception object, such as the values of relevant variables or the state of the application at the time of the exception. This can be helpful for debugging and troubleshooting.

- Handle exceptions at the appropriate level: Catch and handle exceptions at the appropriate level of your code. Avoid catching exceptions too early or too late, as this can make it difficult to determine the cause of the exception and handle it effectively.

By following these best practices, you can ensure that your exceptions are meaningful, informative, and help to improve the overall quality and reliability of your code.

Conclusion

In this section, we learned how to throw exceptions in C#. We explored the throw statement and saw how to throw both built-in and custom exceptions. We also discussed exception propagation and best practices for throwing exceptions. By understanding how to throw exceptions effectively, you can improve the error handling and reliability of your C# applications.

7.4 Custom Exceptions

In C#, exceptions are a powerful mechanism for handling errors and abnormal conditions in your code. While C# provides a wide range of built-in exception classes, there may be situations where you need to create your own custom exceptions to handle specific scenarios in your application. Custom exceptions allow you to provide more meaningful and specific information about the error that occurred, making it easier to debug and troubleshoot your code.

7.4.1 Creating Custom Exceptions

To create a custom exception in C#, you need to define a new class that derives from the base class Exception or one of its derived classes. The Exception class provides a set of properties and methods that are useful for handling and propagating exceptions. By creating a custom exception class, you can add additional properties and methods that are specific to your application's needs.

Here's an example of how to create a custom exception class:

```
public class CustomException : Exception
{
public CustomException() { }
public CustomException(string message) : base(message) { }
public CustomException(string message, Exception innerException) : base(message, innerException) { }
// Add any additional properties or methods here
}
```

In the above example, the CustomException class derives from the Exception class and provides three constructors. The first constructor takes no arguments, the second constructor takes a string message as an argument, and the third constructor takes both a message and an inner exception as arguments. These constructors allow you to provide different levels of information when throwing the custom exception.

7.4.2 Throwing Custom Exceptions

Once you have defined your custom exception class, you can throw instances of it using the throw keyword. Throwing a custom exception allows you to indicate that a specific error condition has occurred in your code.

Here's an example of how to throw a custom exception:

```
public class CustomException : Exception
{
public CustomException(string message) : base(message) { }
}
public class MyClass
{
public void DoSomething()
{
// Some code here
throw new CustomException("An error occurred while doing something.");
// More code here
}
}
```

In the above example, the DoSomething method in the MyClass class throws a CustomException when an error occurs. The throw keyword is followed by the instantiation of the CustomException class with a specific error message. This allows the caller of the DoSomething method to catch and handle the custom exception appropriately.

7.4.3 Catching Custom Exceptions

To catch a custom exception, you can use a try-catch block. The try block contains the code that may throw an exception, and the catch block handles the exception if it occurs.

Here's an example of how to catch a custom exception:

```
public class CustomException : Exception
{
public CustomException(string message) : base(message) { }
```

```
}
public class MyClass
{
public void DoSomething()
{
try
{
// Some code here
throw new CustomException("An error occurred while doing
something.");
// More code here
}
catch (CustomException ex)
{
// Handle the custom exception here
Console.WriteLine(ex.Message);
}
}
}
```

In the above example, the catch block catches the CustomException and handles it by printing the error message to the console. This allows you to provide specific error handling logic for the custom exception.

7.4.4 Best Practices for Custom Exceptions

When creating custom exceptions, it's important to follow some best practices to ensure that your code is maintainable and easy to understand. Here are some guidelines to consider:

1. **Keep it simple**: Only add properties and methods that are necessary for handling the specific error condition. Avoid adding unnecessary complexity to your custom exception class.

2. **Provide meaningful error messages**: The error message

should clearly describe the error condition that occurred. This will make it easier for developers to understand and troubleshoot the issue.

3. **Inherit from existing exception classes**: If your custom exception is similar to an existing exception class, consider deriving from that class instead of the base Exception class. This can provide additional context and functionality specific to the error condition.

4. **Throw exceptions at the appropriate level**: Only throw exceptions when necessary and at the appropriate level of your code. Avoid throwing exceptions for expected or recoverable conditions.

5. **Document your custom exceptions**: Provide documentation for your custom exception classes, including information

6. 8

7. File Handling

8 - File Handling

8.1 Reading and Writing Files

In this section, we will explore how to read and write files in C#. File handling is an essential aspect of programming as it allows us to interact with external files, such as text files, CSV files, XML files, and more. Whether you need to read data from a file or write data to a file, C# provides a rich set of classes and methods to accomplish these tasks efficiently.

8.1.1 Reading Files

To read data from a file in C#, we can use the StreamReader class. This class provides methods for reading characters, lines, or even the entire content of a file. Here's an example of how to read a text file using StreamReader:

```
string filePath = "path/to/file.txt";
using (StreamReader reader = new StreamReader(filePath))
{
string line;
while ((line = reader.ReadLine()) != null)
{
Console.WriteLine(line);
}
}
```

In the above code, we first specify the path to the file we want to read using the filePath variable. Then, we create an instance of the StreamReader class and pass the file path to its constructor. The using statement ensures that the StreamReader is properly disposed of after we finish reading the file.

Inside the using block, we use the ReadLine() method of the StreamReader to read each line of the file. The method returns null when there are no more lines to read. We then print each line to the console using Console.WriteLine().

8.1.2 Writing Files

To write data to a file in C#, we can use the StreamWriter class. This class provides methods for writing characters, lines, or even the entire content to a file. Here's an example of how to write to a text file using StreamWriter:

```
string filePath = "path/to/file.txt";
using (StreamWriter writer = new StreamWriter(filePath))
{
writer.WriteLine("Hello, World!");
writer.WriteLine("This is a sample text.");
}
```

In the above code, we first specify the path to the file we want to write to using the filePath variable. Then, we create an instance of the StreamWriter class and pass the file path to its constructor. The using statement ensures that the StreamWriter is properly disposed of after we finish writing to the file.

Inside the using block, we use the WriteLine() method of the StreamWriter to write each line of text to the file. The method automatically appends a newline character after each line.

8.1.3 File Modes

When working with files, it's important to understand the different file modes available in C#. The file mode determines how the file is opened and whether it can be read from, written to, or both. Here are the commonly used file modes:

- FileMode.Create: Creates a new file. If the file already exists, it will be overwritten.
- FileMode.Open: Opens an existing file. If the file doesn't exist, an exception is thrown.
- FileMode.Append: Opens an existing file or creates a new file if it doesn't exist. The data is appended to the end of the file.
- FileMode.Truncate: Opens an existing file and truncates its content. If the file doesn't exist, an exception is thrown.

You can specify the file mode when creating an instance of the StreamWriter or StreamReader class. For example:

```
using (StreamWriter writer = new StreamWriter(filePath,
FileMode.Append))
{
// Write data to the file
}
using (StreamReader reader = new StreamReader(filePath,
FileMode.Open))
{
// Read data from the file
}
```

8.1.4 File Paths

When working with files, it's important to provide the correct file path. The file path can be either an absolute path or a relative path. An absolute path specifies the full path to the file, starting from the root directory. A relative path specifies the path relative to the current working directory of the application.

Here are some examples of file paths:

- Absolute path: "C:\path\to\file.txt"
- Relative path: "..\folder\file.txt"

You can use the Path class in C# to manipulate file paths and perform operations such as combining paths, getting the file name, extension, and more.

8.1.5 Exception Handling

When working with files, it's important to handle exceptions that may occur. File-related operations can throw exceptions if the file is not found, the file is already in use, or if there are permission issues. To handle exceptions, you can use try-catch blocks. Here's an example:

```
try
{
```

```
using (StreamReader reader = new StreamReader(filePath))
{
// Read data from the file
}
}
catch (FileNotFoundException ex)
{
Console.WriteLine("File not found: " + ex.Message);
}
catch (IOException ex)
{
Console.WriteLine("An error occurred while reading the file: " +
ex.Message);
}
```

In the above code, we use a try-catch block to catch specific exceptions that may occur during file reading. If a FileNotFoundException is thrown, we print a custom error message. If an IOException is thrown, we print a different error message. You can catch other specific exceptions or use a more general Exception catch block to handle any other exceptions that may occur.

Conclusion

In this section, we learned how to read and write files in C#. We explored the StreamReader and StreamWriter classes, file modes, file paths, and exception handling. File handling is a crucial skill for any C# developer, as it allows you to work with external data and persist information. With the knowledge gained in this section, you can confidently handle file operations in your C# applications.

8.2 Working with Directories

In this section, we will explore how to work with directories in C#. A directory, also known as a folder, is a container that holds files and other directories. Understanding how to create, navigate, and manipulate directories is essential for managing files and organizing data in your C# applications.

8.2.1 Creating Directories

To create a new directory in C#, you can use the Directory.CreateDirectory() method. This method takes a string parameter representing the path of the directory you want to create. The path can be either an absolute path or a relative path.

Here's an example that demonstrates how to create a new directory:

```
string path = @"C:\MyDirectory";
Directory.CreateDirectory(path);
```

In this example, we create a new directory named "MyDirectory" in the root of the C drive. If the directory already exists, the method will do nothing.

8.2.2 Checking if a Directory Exists

Before creating a directory, it's a good practice to check if it already exists. You can use the Directory.Exists() method to determine if a directory exists at a given path. This method returns a boolean value indicating whether the directory exists or not.

Here's an example that demonstrates how to check if a directory exists:

```
string path = @"C:\MyDirectory";
if (Directory.Exists(path))
{
Console.WriteLine("The directory already exists.");
}
else
```

```
{
Console.WriteLine("The directory does not exist.");
}
```

In this example, we check if the directory "MyDirectory" exists in the root of the C drive. If it exists, we display a message indicating that the directory already exists. Otherwise, we display a message indicating that the directory does not exist.

8.2.3 Getting the Contents of a Directory

To get the contents of a directory, you can use the Directory.GetFiles() and Directory.GetDirectories() methods. The GetFiles() method returns an array of strings representing the file names in the specified directory, while the GetDirectories() method returns an array of strings representing the directory names in the specified directory.

Here's an example that demonstrates how to get the contents of a directory:

```
string path = @"C:\MyDirectory";
string[] files = Directory.GetFiles(path);
string[] directories = Directory.GetDirectories(path);
Console.WriteLine("Files:");
foreach (string file in files)
{
Console.WriteLine(file);
}
Console.WriteLine("Directories:");
foreach (string directory in directories)
{
Console.WriteLine(directory);
}
```

In this example, we get the contents of the directory "MyDirectory" in the root of the C drive. We then iterate over the arrays of file names and directory names and display them on the console.

8.2.4 Deleting a Directory

To delete a directory, you can use the Directory.Delete() method. This method takes a string parameter representing the path of the directory you want to delete. By default, the method will only delete empty directories. If you want to delete a directory and its contents, you can pass true as the second parameter.

Here's an example that demonstrates how to delete a directory:

```
string path = @"C:\MyDirectory";
Directory.Delete(path);
```

In this example, we delete the directory "MyDirectory" in the root of the C drive. If the directory is not empty, an exception will be thrown. To delete a directory and its contents, you can use the following code:

```
string path = @"C:\MyDirectory";
Directory.Delete(path, true);
```

8.2.5 Moving and Renaming Directories

To move a directory to a new location or rename it, you can use the Directory.Move() method. This method takes two string parameters: the current path of the directory and the new path or name.

Here's an example that demonstrates how to move and rename a directory:

```
string currentPath = @"C:\MyDirectory";
string newPath = @"D:\NewDirectory";
Directory.Move(currentPath, newPath);
```

In this example, we move the directory "MyDirectory" from the C drive to the D drive and rename it to "NewDirectory". If the destination directory already exists, an exception will be thrown.

8.2.6 Working with Directory Information

The DirectoryInfo class provides a more object-oriented approach to working with directories. It encapsulates information and operations related to a directory. You can create a DirectoryInfo object by passing the path of the directory to its constructor.

Here's an example that demonstrates how to use the DirectoryInfo class:

```
string path = @"C:\MyDirectory";
DirectoryInfo directoryInfo = new DirectoryInfo(path);
Console.WriteLine("Directory Name: " + directoryInfo.Name);
Console.WriteLine("Parent Directory: " + directoryInfo.Parent);
Console.WriteLine("Creation          Time:        "         +
directoryInfo.CreationTime);
Console.WriteLine("Last        Write        Time:       "       +
directoryInfo.LastWriteTime);
```

In this example, we create a DirectoryInfo object for the directory "MyDirectory" in the root of the C drive. We then access various properties of the DirectoryInfo object, such as the directory name, parent directory, creation time, and last write time.

Conclusion

Working with directories is an essential part of managing files and organizing data in your C# applications. In this section, we explored how to create directories, check if they exist, get their contents, delete them, move and rename them, and work with directory information using the built-in classes and methods provided by the .NET Framework.

8.3 File and Directory Manipulation

In this section, we will explore the various operations that can be performed on files and directories using C#. File and directory manipulation is an essential aspect of any programming language, as it allows us to create, read, write, delete, and manage files and directories on the computer's file system.

8.3.1 Working with Files

C# provides a rich set of classes and methods to work with files. The System.IO namespace contains classes such as File and FileInfo that allow us to perform various file-related operations.

To create a new file, we can use the File.Create() method. This method returns a FileStream object that can be used to write data to the file. We can also use the File.WriteAllText() method to create a new file and write text to it in a single line of code.

```
string filePath = @"C:\MyFiles\sample.txt";
// Create a new file
File.Create(filePath);
// Write text to the file
File.WriteAllText(filePath, "Hello, World!");
```

To read the contents of a file, we can use the File.ReadAllText() method, which returns the contents of the file as a string. Alternatively, we can use the File.ReadAllLines() method to read the contents of a file line by line and store them in an array of strings.

```
string filePath = @"C:\MyFiles\sample.txt";
// Read the entire file
string fileContents = File.ReadAllText(filePath);
// Read the file line by line
string[] lines = File.ReadAllLines(filePath);
```

To append text to an existing file, we can use the File.AppendAllText() method. This method appends the specified text to the end of the file.

```
string filePath = @"C:\MyFiles\sample.txt";
// Append text to the file
File.AppendAllText(filePath, "This is a new line.");
```

To copy a file from one location to another, we can use the File.Copy() method. This method takes two parameters: the source file path and the destination file path.

```
string sourceFilePath = @"C:\MyFiles\sample.txt";
string destinationFilePath = @"C:\Backup\sample.txt";
// Copy the file
File.Copy(sourceFilePath, destinationFilePath);
```

To move a file from one location to another, we can use the File.Move() method. This method takes two parameters: the source file path and the destination file path.

```
string sourceFilePath = @"C:\MyFiles\sample.txt";
string destinationFilePath = @"C:\Archive\sample.txt";
// Move the file
File.Move(sourceFilePath, destinationFilePath);
```

To delete a file, we can use the File.Delete() method. This method deletes the specified file from the file system.

```
string filePath = @"C:\MyFiles\sample.txt";
// Delete the file
File.Delete(filePath);
```

8.3.2 Working with Directories

C# provides several classes and methods to work with directories. The System.IO namespace contains classes such as Directory and DirectoryInfo that allow us to perform various directory-related operations.

To create a new directory, we can use the Directory.CreateDirectory() method. This method creates a new directory at the specified path.

```
string directoryPath = @"C:\MyFiles\NewDirectory";
// Create a new directory
```

```
Directory.CreateDirectory(directoryPath);
```

To check if a directory exists, we can use the Directory.Exists() method. This method returns true if the directory exists, and false otherwise.

```
string directoryPath = @"C:\MyFiles\ExistingDirectory";
// Check if the directory exists
if (Directory.Exists(directoryPath))
{
Console.WriteLine("The directory exists.");
}
else
{
Console.WriteLine("The directory does not exist.");
}
```

To get the files in a directory, we can use the Directory.GetFiles() method. This method returns an array of strings containing the paths of all the files in the specified directory.

```
string directoryPath = @"C:\MyFiles";
// Get the files in the directory
string[] files = Directory.GetFiles(directoryPath);
foreach (string file in files)
{
Console.WriteLine(file);
}
```

To get the subdirectories in a directory, we can use the Directory.GetDirectories() method. This method returns an array of strings containing the paths of all the subdirectories in the specified directory.

```
string directoryPath = @"C:\MyFiles";
// Get the subdirectories in the directory
string[] subdirectories = Directory.GetDirectories(directoryPath);
foreach (string subdirectory in subdirectories)
```

```
{
Console.WriteLine(subdirectory);
}
```

To delete a directory, we can use the Directory.Delete() method. This method deletes the specified directory from the file system. By default, this method only deletes empty directories. To delete a directory and its contents, we can pass true as the second parameter.

```
string directoryPath = @"C:\MyFiles\EmptyDirectory";
// Delete the directory
Directory.Delete(directoryPath);
string      directoryPathWithContents      =      @"C:\MyFiles\
DirectoryWithContents";
// Delete the directory and its contents
Directory.Delete(directoryPathWithContents, true);
```

8.3.3 Summary

In this section, we explored the various file and directory manipulation operations available in C#. We learned how to create, read, write, delete, copy, and move files, as well as create, check, and delete directories. Understanding these operations is crucial for any C# developer who needs to work with files and directories in their applications.

8.4 Serialization and Deserialization

Serialization and deserialization are important concepts in C# that allow you to convert objects into a format that can be stored or transmitted, and then convert them back into objects when needed. This process is commonly used in scenarios such as saving and loading data, sending objects over a network, or storing objects in a database. In this section, we will explore how to perform serialization and deserialization in C#.

8.4.1 Introduction to Serialization

Serialization is the process of converting an object into a stream of bytes so that it can be stored or transmitted. This stream of bytes can then be used to recreate the object at a later time. The .NET framework provides built-in support for serialization through the System.Runtime.Serialization namespace.

To make an object serializable, you need to mark it with the [Serializable] attribute. This attribute tells the .NET runtime that the object can be serialized. By default, all public and private fields of the object will be serialized. However, you can control the serialization process by using attributes such as [NonSerialized] to exclude specific fields from serialization.

8.4.2 Serializing Objects

To serialize an object, you need to create an instance of the BinaryFormatter class from the System.Runtime.Serialization.Formatters.Binary namespace. This class provides methods for serializing and deserializing objects.

Here's an example of how to serialize an object:

```
using System;
using System.IO;
using System.Runtime.Serialization.Formatters.Binary;
[Serializable]
public class Person
```

```
{
public string Name { get; set; }
public int Age { get; set; }
}
public class Program
{
public static void Main()
{
Person person = new Person { Name = "John Doe", Age = 30 };
BinaryFormatter formatter = new BinaryFormatter();
using (FileStream stream = new FileStream("person.dat",
FileMode.Create))
{
formatter.Serialize(stream, person);
}
}
}
```

In this example, we create an instance of the Person class and set its properties. We then create an instance of the BinaryFormatter class and use it to serialize the person object into a file called "person.dat".

8.4.3 Deserializing Objects

Deserialization is the process of recreating an object from a stream of bytes. To deserialize an object, you need to use the BinaryFormatter class again, but this time you call the Deserialize method instead of Serialize.

Here's an example of how to deserialize an object:

```
using System;
using System.IO;
using System.Runtime.Serialization.Formatters.Binary;
[Serializable]
public class Person
{
```

```
public string Name { get; set; }
public int Age { get; set; }
}
public class Program
{
public static void Main()
{
Person person;
BinaryFormatter formatter = new BinaryFormatter();
using (FileStream stream = new FileStream("person.dat",
FileMode.Open))
{
person = (Person)formatter.Deserialize(stream);
}
Console.WriteLine($"Name:        {person.Name},        Age:
{person.Age}");
}
}
```

In this example, we create an instance of the Person class and deserialize it from the "person.dat" file. We cast the deserialized object to the Person type and then access its properties to display the name and age.

8.4.4 Customizing Serialization

Sometimes, you may need to customize the serialization process for certain objects. You can do this by implementing the ISerializable interface in your class. This interface provides two methods: GetObjectData, which is responsible for serializing the object, and a constructor that takes a SerializationInfo object and a StreamingContext object, which is responsible for deserializing the object.

Here's an example of how to customize serialization:

```
using System;
```

```csharp
using System.IO;
using System.Runtime.Serialization;
using System.Runtime.Serialization.Formatters.Binary;
[Serializable]
public class Person : ISerializable
{
public string Name { get; set; }
public int Age { get; set; }
public Person() { }
protected Person(SerializationInfo info, StreamingContext context)
{
Name = info.GetString("Name");
Age = info.GetInt32("Age");
}
public void GetObjectData(SerializationInfo info, StreamingContext context)
{
info.AddValue("Name", Name);
info.AddValue("Age", Age);
}
}
public class Program
{
public static void Main()
{
Person person = new Person { Name = "John Doe", Age = 30 };
BinaryFormatter formatter = new BinaryFormatter();
using (FileStream stream = new FileStream("person.dat", FileMode.Create))
{
formatter.Serialize(stream, person);
```

```
    }
  }
}
```

In this example, we implement the ISerializable interface in the Person class. We provide an implementation for the GetObjectData method to specify which fields should be serialized. In the constructor that takes a SerializationInfo object, we retrieve the serialized values and assign them to the corresponding properties.

8.4.5 Serialization Best Practices

When working with serialization, there are a few best practices to keep in mind:

- Mark all serializable classes with the [Serializable] attribute.
- Avoid serializing sensitive data such as passwords or encryption keys.
- Be cautious when serializing objects with circular references, as it can lead to infinite loops during deserialization.
- Test the serialization and deserialization process thoroughly to ensure data integrity.

Serialization and deserialization are powerful techniques that allow you to persist and transfer objects in C#. By understanding how to serialize and deserialize objects, you can effectively store and retrieve data, making your applications more flexible and robust.

9 - Working with Databases

9.1 Introduction to Databases

In today's digital age, data is at the heart of every application. Whether it's a simple to-do list or a complex enterprise system, the ability to store, retrieve, and manipulate data is crucial. This is where databases come into play. A database is a structured collection of data that is organized and managed in a way that allows for efficient storage, retrieval, and manipulation.

9.1.1 What is a Database?

A database is a software system that is designed to store, manage, and retrieve large amounts of data. It provides a structured way to organize and store data, making it easy to access and manipulate. Databases are used in a wide range of applications, from small personal projects to large enterprise systems.

9.1.2 Types of Databases

There are several types of databases, each designed for specific use cases. The most common types of databases are:

1. Relational Databases: Relational databases are the most widely used type of database. They store data in tables, with each table consisting of rows and columns. Relational databases use a structured query language (SQL) to interact with the data. Examples of relational databases include MySQL, Oracle, and Microsoft SQL Server.

2. NoSQL Databases: NoSQL databases, also known as non-relational databases, are designed to handle large amounts of unstructured or semi-structured data. Unlike relational databases, NoSQL databases do not use tables and SQL. Instead, they use different data models, such as key-value, document, columnar, or graph. Examples of NoSQL databases include MongoDB, Cassandra, and Redis.

3. Object-Oriented Databases: Object-oriented databases are

designed to store and manage objects, which are instances of classes in object-oriented programming. These databases provide support for object-oriented concepts such as inheritance, encapsulation, and polymorphism. Examples of object-oriented databases include db4o and ObjectDB.

4. Graph Databases: Graph databases are designed to store and manage graph-like structures, where data is represented as nodes and edges. These databases are particularly useful for applications that involve complex relationships and network analysis. Examples of graph databases include Neo4j and Amazon Neptune.

9.1.3 Benefits of Using Databases

Using a database to store and manage data offers several benefits:

1. Data Integrity: Databases provide mechanisms to ensure data integrity, such as enforcing data constraints and implementing referential integrity. This helps maintain the accuracy and consistency of the data.

2. Data Security: Databases offer built-in security features to protect sensitive data. Access control mechanisms can be implemented to restrict unauthorized access to the data.

3. Data Scalability: Databases are designed to handle large amounts of data and can scale horizontally or vertically to accommodate growing data needs. This allows applications to handle increasing workloads without sacrificing performance.

4. Data Consistency: Databases provide transactional support, which ensures that data modifications are atomic, consistent, isolated, and durable (ACID). This guarantees that data remains consistent even in the presence of concurrent operations or system failures.

5. Data Retrieval and Manipulation: Databases provide powerful query languages, such as SQL, that allow for

efficient retrieval and manipulation of data. Complex queries can be executed to extract specific information from the database.

9.1.4 Database Management Systems (DBMS)

A Database Management System (DBMS) is a software system that provides an interface to interact with databases. It allows users to create, modify, and query databases without having to deal with the underlying complexities of data storage and retrieval. DBMSs provide tools and utilities to manage databases, including backup and recovery, performance tuning, and security management.

Some popular DBMSs include:

1. MySQL: MySQL is an open-source relational database management system that is widely used for web applications. It is known for its speed, reliability, and ease of use.
2. Microsoft SQL Server: Microsoft SQL Server is a relational database management system developed by Microsoft. It is commonly used in enterprise environments and offers a wide range of features and tools.
3. Oracle Database: Oracle Database is a powerful and scalable relational database management system. It is widely used in enterprise applications and offers advanced features for data management and performance optimization.
4. MongoDB: MongoDB is a popular NoSQL database that stores data in a flexible, JSON-like format. It is known for its scalability, high performance, and ease of use.

9.1.5 Conclusion

Databases are an essential component of modern software development. They provide a structured and efficient way to store, retrieve, and manipulate data. Understanding the basics of databases is crucial for any developer working with data-driven applications. In the next section, we will explore how to connect to a database and perform basic operations using C#.

9.2 Connecting to a Database

In today's digital age, data is the lifeblood of many applications. Whether it's storing user information, managing inventory, or analyzing customer behavior, databases play a crucial role in the functionality of modern software systems. In this section, we will explore how to connect to a database using C# and perform various operations on the data.

9.2.1 Introduction to Database Connectivity

Before we dive into the specifics of connecting to a database, let's first understand the concept of database connectivity. In simple terms, database connectivity refers to the ability of a program to establish a connection with a database management system (DBMS) and interact with the data stored within it. This interaction can involve querying the database for information, inserting new records, updating existing data, or deleting records.

In C#, there are several ways to connect to a database, but the most common approach is to use the ADO.NET framework. ADO.NET provides a set of classes and libraries that enable developers to interact with various database systems, such as Microsoft SQL Server, MySQL, Oracle, and more. By leveraging ADO.NET, you can establish a connection to a database, execute SQL queries, and retrieve or modify data.

9.2.2 Establishing a Database Connection

To connect to a database using C#, you need to provide the necessary connection details, such as the server name, database name, username, and password. Once you have these details, you can use the SqlConnection class from the System.Data.SqlClient namespace to establish a connection. Here's an example:

```
using System;
using System.Data.SqlClient;
namespace DatabaseConnectivity
```

```
{
class Program
{
static void Main(string[] args)
{
string                    connectionString                =
"Server=myServerAddress;Database=myDatabase;User
Id=myUsername;Password=myPassword;";
using       (SqlConnection      connection      =      new
SqlConnection(connectionString))
{
try
{
connection.Open();
Console.WriteLine("Connection successful!");
}
catch (Exception ex)
{
Console.WriteLine("Error  connecting  to  the  database:  " +
ex.Message);
}
}
}
}
}
```

In the above code snippet, we create a SqlConnection object and pass the connection string as a parameter to its constructor. The connection string contains the necessary information to establish a connection to the database. We then use the Open() method to open the connection. If the connection is successful, we display a success message; otherwise, we catch any exceptions that occur and display an error message.

9.2.3 Executing SQL Queries

Once you have established a connection to the database, you can execute SQL queries to retrieve or modify data. A SQL query is a statement written in the Structured Query Language (SQL) that instructs the database to perform a specific operation. In C#, you can use the SqlCommand class to execute SQL queries. Here's an example:

```csharp
using System;
using System.Data.SqlClient;
namespace DatabaseConnectivity
{
class Program
{
static void Main(string[] args)
{
string                    connectionString             =
"Server=myServerAddress;Database=myDatabase;User
Id=myUsername;Password=myPassword;";
using       (SqlConnection       connection       =       new
SqlConnection(connectionString))
{
try
{
connection.Open();
Console.WriteLine("Connection successful!");
string sqlQuery = "SELECT * FROM Customers";
SqlCommand   command   =   new   SqlCommand(sqlQuery,
connection);
SqlDataReader reader = command.ExecuteReader();
while (reader.Read())
{
Console.WriteLine("Customer Name: " + reader["Name"]);
}
```

```
reader.Close();
}
catch (Exception ex)
{
Console.WriteLine("Error executing SQL query: " + ex.Message);
}
}
}
}
}
```

In the above code snippet, we first establish a connection to the database using the SqlConnection class. We then create a SqlCommand object and pass the SQL query and the connection object as parameters to its constructor. We use the ExecuteReader() method to execute the query and retrieve the results. Finally, we iterate over the results using the Read() method of the SqlDataReader class and display the customer names.

9.2.4 Working with Data

In addition to executing SQL queries, ADO.NET provides various classes and methods to work with data retrieved from the database. For example, you can use the ExecuteNonQuery() method of the SqlCommand class to execute SQL statements that do not return any data, such as INSERT, UPDATE, or DELETE statements. You can also use the ExecuteScalar() method to retrieve a single value from the database, such as the count of records or the maximum value of a column.

Furthermore, ADO.NET allows you to work with data in a disconnected manner. This means that you can retrieve data from the database, disconnect from the database, and then manipulate the data locally without maintaining an active connection. This can be useful when working with large datasets or when performing complex data manipulations.

Conclusion

Connecting to a database is a fundamental skill for any C# developer. By leveraging the ADO.NET framework, you can establish connections, execute SQL queries, and work with data in a flexible and efficient manner. In this section, we explored the basics of connecting to a database using C# and executing SQL queries. In the next section, we will delve deeper into executing more complex queries and working with data in a more advanced manner.

9.3 Executing SQL Queries

In this section, we will explore how to execute SQL queries in C#. SQL (Structured Query Language) is a standard language for managing and manipulating relational databases. It allows us to perform various operations such as creating tables, inserting data, updating records, and retrieving data from the database.

To execute SQL queries in C#, we need to establish a connection to the database using the appropriate provider. There are several database providers available for C#, such as SQL Server, MySQL, Oracle, and SQLite. Each provider has its own set of classes and methods for executing SQL queries.

9.3.1 Connecting to the Database

Before executing SQL queries, we need to establish a connection to the database. The connection provides a channel for communication between the application and the database. To connect to a database, we need to provide the necessary connection string, which contains information such as the server name, database name, username, and password.

Here is an example of connecting to a SQL Server database using the SqlConnection class:

```
string connectionString = "Data Source=serverName;Initial Catalog=databaseName;User ID=userName;Password=password";

SqlConnection connection = new SqlConnection(connectionString);

connection.Open();
```

In the above code, we create a connection string with the appropriate values for the server name, database name, username, and password. Then, we create an instance of the SqlConnection class and pass the connection string as a parameter to the constructor. Finally, we call the Open() method to establish the connection to the database.

9.3.2 Executing SQL Queries

Once we have established a connection to the database, we can execute SQL queries using the SqlCommand class. The SqlCommand class provides methods for executing different types of SQL queries, such as SELECT, INSERT, UPDATE, and DELETE.

Here is an example of executing a SELECT query to retrieve data from a table:

```
string query = "SELECT * FROM Customers";
SqlCommand command = new SqlCommand(query, connection);
SqlDataReader reader = command.ExecuteReader();
while (reader.Read())
{
// Process the retrieved data
string customerId = reader["CustomerID"].ToString();
string companyName = reader["CompanyName"].ToString();
// ...
}
reader.Close();
```

In the above code, we create a SQL query string to select all records from the Customers table. Then, we create an instance of the SqlCommand class and pass the query string and the connection object as parameters to the constructor. We call the ExecuteReader() method to execute the query and retrieve the data.

The ExecuteReader() method returns a SqlDataReader object, which allows us to iterate over the retrieved data using the Read() method. Inside the while loop, we can access the values of each column using the column name or index.

9.3.3 Parameterized Queries

When executing SQL queries, it is important to use parameterized queries to prevent SQL injection attacks and improve performance. Parameterized queries allow us to pass values to the query as parameters, rather than concatenating them directly into the query string.

Here is an example of executing a parameterized query:

string query = "SELECT * FROM Customers WHERE Country = @Country";

SqlCommand command = new SqlCommand(query, connection);

command.Parameters.AddWithValue("@Country", "USA");

SqlDataReader reader = command.ExecuteReader();

while (reader.Read())

{

// Process the retrieved data

string customerId = reader["CustomerID"].ToString();

string companyName = reader["CompanyName"].ToString();

// ...

}

reader.Close();

In the above code, we use the @Country parameter in the query string and pass the actual value "USA" using the Parameters.AddWithValue() method. This ensures that the value is properly escaped and prevents any potential SQL injection attacks.

9.3.4 Executing Non-Query Statements

In addition to SELECT queries, we can also execute non-query statements such as INSERT, UPDATE, and DELETE using the ExecuteNonQuery() method of the SqlCommand class. This method is used when we don't expect any result set to be returned from the query.

Here is an example of executing an INSERT query:

string query = "INSERT INTO Customers (CustomerID, CompanyName) VALUES (@CustomerID, @CompanyName)";

SqlCommand command = new SqlCommand(query, connection);

command.Parameters.AddWithValue("@CustomerID", "12345");

command.Parameters.AddWithValue("@CompanyName", "ABC Company");

int rowsAffected = command.ExecuteNonQuery();

In the above code, we use the INSERT statement to insert a new record into the Customers table. We pass the values for the CustomerID and CompanyName columns as parameters using the Parameters.AddWithValue() method. The ExecuteNonQuery() method returns the number of rows affected by the query.

9.3.5 Error Handling

When executing SQL queries, it is important to handle any errors that may occur during the execution. The SqlCommand class provides a Try-Catch block to catch and handle any exceptions that may be thrown.

Here is an example of error handling when executing a query:

```
try
{
// Execute SQL query
}
catch (SqlException ex)
{
// Handle SQL exception
Console.WriteLine("An error occurred: " + ex.Message);
}
finally
{
// Close the connection
connection.Close();
}
```

In the above code, we wrap the execution of the SQL query inside a Try block. If an exception occurs, it is caught in the Catch block, where we can handle the exception and display an appropriate error message.

Finally, we close the connection in the Finally block to ensure that the resources are properly released.

Conclusion

Executing SQL queries in C# allows us to interact with databases and retrieve or modify data. In this section, we learned how to establish a connection to the database, execute SQL queries using the SqlCommand class, use parameterized queries to prevent SQL injection attacks, execute non-query statements, and handle errors that may occur during the execution. By mastering these techniques, you will be able to effectively work with databases in your C# applications.

9.4 Working with Data

In this section, we will explore how to work with data in C#. Data is a fundamental aspect of any application, and understanding how to manipulate and manage data is crucial for building robust and efficient software.

9.4.1 Introduction to Data Manipulation

Data manipulation refers to the process of retrieving, modifying, and storing data in a database. In C#, we can interact with databases using various techniques and frameworks, such as ADO.NET, Entity Framework, or third-party libraries.

When working with data, it is essential to understand the underlying concepts and principles. This includes understanding database management systems, SQL (Structured Query Language), and data modeling.

9.4.2 Connecting to a Database

Before we can work with data, we need to establish a connection to the database. In C#, we can use the ADO.NET framework to connect to various database systems, such as SQL Server, MySQL, or Oracle.

To establish a connection, we need to provide the necessary connection string, which contains information about the database server, credentials, and other connection parameters. Once the connection is established, we can execute SQL queries and retrieve data from the database.

9.4.3 Executing SQL Queries

SQL (Structured Query Language) is a standard language for interacting with relational databases. In C#, we can execute SQL queries using ADO.NET's SqlCommand class.

To execute a query, we first create an instance of the SqlCommand class and pass the SQL query as a string parameter. We can then execute the query using the ExecuteNonQuery, ExecuteScalar, or

ExecuteReader methods, depending on the type of query and the expected result.

Executing SQL queries allows us to perform various operations on the database, such as retrieving data, inserting records, updating existing records, or deleting records.

9.4.4 Retrieving Data

Retrieving data from a database is a common task in many applications. In C#, we can use the SqlDataReader class to retrieve data from a database after executing a SELECT query.

After executing the query, the SqlDataReader provides methods to iterate over the result set and retrieve the data. We can access the data by specifying the column name or index.

It is important to handle exceptions and close the SqlDataReader and database connection properly to avoid resource leaks and ensure the efficient use of system resources.

9.4.5 Modifying Data

Modifying data in a database involves performing operations such as inserting, updating, or deleting records. In C#, we can use the SqlCommand class to execute SQL queries that modify the data in the database.

To insert records, we can use the INSERT INTO statement and provide the necessary values for each column. To update records, we can use the UPDATE statement and specify the columns to be updated and the new values. To delete records, we can use the DELETE statement and specify the condition for the records to be deleted.

It is important to handle exceptions and ensure proper error handling when modifying data to maintain data integrity and avoid unintended consequences.

9.4.6 Transactions

Transactions are used to ensure the atomicity, consistency, isolation, and durability (ACID) properties of database operations.

In C#, we can use the System.Transactions namespace to work with transactions.

Transactions allow us to group multiple database operations into a single unit of work. If any operation within the transaction fails, all the changes made within the transaction can be rolled back, ensuring that the database remains in a consistent state.

To work with transactions, we can use the TransactionScope class, which provides a simple and intuitive way to define and manage transactions in C#.

9.4.7 Data Validation and Sanitization

When working with data, it is crucial to validate and sanitize the input to ensure data integrity and prevent security vulnerabilities such as SQL injection attacks.

Data validation involves checking the input data against predefined rules or constraints to ensure that it meets the required criteria. This can include checking for data types, length limits, format validation, and business rules.

Data sanitization involves removing or escaping any potentially harmful characters or sequences from the input data to prevent SQL injection or other security vulnerabilities.

C# provides various techniques and libraries for data validation and sanitization, such as regular expressions, parameterized queries, and input validation libraries.

9.4.8 Data Access Layer

To improve code organization and maintainability, it is common to separate the data access logic from the rest of the application code. This is typically done by creating a data access layer (DAL) that encapsulates the database operations.

The DAL provides a set of methods or classes that abstract the underlying database operations, making it easier to work with data in the application code. It also allows for better separation of concerns and promotes code reuse.

In C#, we can create a DAL using various techniques, such as using ADO.NET directly, using an ORM (Object-Relational Mapping) framework like Entity Framework, or implementing a custom data access layer.

9.4.9 Working with Data in C# Frameworks

C# provides several frameworks and libraries that simplify working with data. Some popular frameworks include Entity Framework, Dapper, and NHibernate.

Entity Framework is an ORM framework that allows developers to work with databases using object-oriented concepts. It provides a high-level abstraction over the database operations and supports various database providers.

Dapper is a lightweight micro-ORM that focuses on performance and simplicity. It provides a simple API for executing SQL queries and mapping the results to objects.

NHibernate is another popular ORM framework that provides advanced features and flexibility. It supports various database providers and offers features like lazy loading, caching, and advanced querying capabilities.

These frameworks can significantly simplify the process of working with data in C# applications and provide additional features like automatic mapping, change tracking, and query optimization.

Conclusion

Working with data is a fundamental aspect of building software applications. In this section, we explored various techniques and concepts related to working with data in C#. We learned how to connect to a database, execute SQL queries, retrieve and modify data, work with transactions, validate and sanitize input, and create a data access layer. We also discussed popular frameworks and libraries that simplify working with data in C#. By mastering these concepts and techniques, you will be well-equipped to handle data-related tasks in your C# applications.

10 - Multithreading

10.1 Introduction to Multithreading

Multithreading is a powerful concept in programming that allows multiple threads of execution to run concurrently within a single program. In simple terms, it enables a program to perform multiple tasks simultaneously, improving performance and responsiveness. In this section, we will explore the fundamentals of multithreading in C# and learn how to create and manage threads, synchronize and lock resources, and ensure thread safety.

10.1.1 What is Multithreading?

Multithreading is the ability of a program to execute multiple threads concurrently. A thread is a lightweight unit of execution within a process. By utilizing multiple threads, a program can perform multiple tasks simultaneously, making efficient use of system resources and improving overall performance.

In a single-threaded program, tasks are executed sequentially, one after another. This means that if a task takes a long time to complete, it can block the execution of subsequent tasks, leading to a delay in the overall program execution. Multithreading solves this problem by allowing tasks to be executed concurrently, ensuring that the program remains responsive even when some tasks are time-consuming.

10.1.2 Benefits of Multithreading

Multithreading offers several benefits in software development:

1. **Improved Performance**: By executing tasks concurrently, multithreading can significantly improve the performance of a program. It allows the program to utilize the available system resources efficiently, making it possible to complete tasks faster.

2. **Responsiveness**: Multithreading ensures that a program remains responsive even when performing time-consuming tasks. By executing these tasks in separate threads, the user

interface remains active and responsive, allowing users to interact with the program without experiencing any delays.

3. **Efficient Resource Utilization**: Multithreading allows a program to make efficient use of system resources, such as CPU cores. By utilizing multiple threads, a program can distribute the workload across multiple cores, maximizing the utilization of available resources.

4. **Parallel Processing**: Multithreading enables parallel processing, where multiple tasks are executed simultaneously. This is particularly useful for computationally intensive tasks, such as data processing or rendering, where dividing the workload among multiple threads can significantly reduce the overall processing time.

10.1.3 Creating and Managing Threads

In C#, creating and managing threads is made easy with the help of the System.Threading namespace. The Thread class provides the necessary functionality to create, start, and manage threads in a C# program.

To create a new thread, you can instantiate the Thread class and pass a method to be executed as a parameter. This method is commonly referred to as the thread's entry point. Once the thread is created, you can start it by calling the Start method. The runtime will then allocate system resources and schedule the thread for execution.

Here's an example of creating and starting a new thread:

```
using System;
using System.Threading;
class Program
{
static void Main()
{
Thread thread = new Thread(DoWork);
thread.Start();
```

```
// Main thread continues executing...
}
static void DoWork()
{
// Code to be executed by the new thread
}
}
```

In this example, a new thread is created by instantiating the Thread class and passing the DoWork method as the thread's entry point. The Start method is then called to start the thread's execution. The main thread continues executing while the new thread runs concurrently.

10.1.4 Synchronization and Locking

When multiple threads access shared resources concurrently, it can lead to race conditions and data corruption. To prevent such issues, synchronization mechanisms are used to ensure that only one thread can access a shared resource at a time.

In C#, the lock statement provides a simple way to synchronize access to shared resources. By enclosing a block of code within a lock statement, you can ensure that only one thread can execute that code block at a time. Other threads attempting to access the same code block will be blocked until the lock is released.

Here's an example of using the lock statement to synchronize access to a shared resource:

```
using System;
using System.Threading;
class Program
{
static int counter = 0;
static object lockObject = new object();
static void Main()
{
Thread thread1 = new Thread(IncrementCounter);
```

```
Thread thread2 = new Thread(IncrementCounter);
thread1.Start();
thread2.Start();
thread1.Join();
thread2.Join();
Console.WriteLine("Counter: " + counter);
}
static void IncrementCounter()
{
for (int i = 0; i < 100000; i++)
{
lock (lockObject)
{
counter++;
}
}
}
}
```

In this example, two threads are created, and both threads increment the counter variable in a loop. The lock statement is used to ensure that only one thread can access the counter variable at a time. Without synchronization, the result would be unpredictable, as both threads could access and modify the counter variable simultaneously.

10.1.5 Thread Safety

Thread safety is an important concept in multithreaded programming. It refers to the ability of a program to function correctly and produce predictable results when multiple threads are executing concurrently.

To ensure thread safety, you need to carefully design your program and use appropriate synchronization mechanisms. This includes properly synchronizing access to shared resources, avoiding race conditions, and using thread-safe data structures and algorithms.

In addition to synchronization, other techniques such as atomic operations, immutable data, and thread-local storage can also be used to achieve thread safety.

It's important to note that achieving thread safety can sometimes come at the cost of performance. Synchronization mechanisms can introduce overhead and potentially reduce the scalability of a multithreaded program. Therefore, it's crucial to strike a balance between thread safety and performance when designing and implementing multithreaded applications.

Conclusion

Multithreading is a powerful technique that allows programs to perform multiple tasks concurrently, improving performance and responsiveness. In this section, we explored the basics of multithreading in C#, including creating and managing threads, synchronizing access to shared resources, and ensuring thread safety. By understanding and applying these concepts, you can harness the full potential of multithreading and build efficient and robust applications.

10.2 Creating and Managing Threads

In C#, a thread is a lightweight unit of execution that can run concurrently with other threads. Threads allow you to perform multiple tasks simultaneously, improving the overall performance and responsiveness of your application. In this section, we will explore how to create and manage threads in C#.

10.2.1 Introduction to Threads

A thread represents an independent flow of execution within a process. Each thread has its own stack, program counter, and set of registers. By default, a C# program starts with a single thread called the main thread. However, you can create additional threads to perform tasks concurrently.

Threads can be used to perform time-consuming operations, such as downloading files, processing large amounts of data, or performing complex calculations, without blocking the main thread. This allows your application to remain responsive and continue executing other tasks while the thread is running.

10.2.2 Creating Threads

In C#, you can create threads using the Thread class from the System.Threading namespace. To create a new thread, you need to define a method that will be executed by the thread. This method is often referred to as the thread's entry point.

Here's an example of creating a new thread:

```
using System;
using System.Threading;
public class Program
{
public static void Main()
{
// Create a new thread and specify the entry point method
Thread thread = new Thread(DoWork);
```

```
// Start the thread
thread.Start();
// Continue executing other tasks on the main thread
Console.WriteLine("Main thread is doing some work...");
// Wait for the thread to complete
thread.Join();
// Continue executing other tasks on the main thread
Console.WriteLine("Main thread has finished.");
}
public static void DoWork()
{
// Perform some time-consuming operation
Console.WriteLine("Thread is doing some work...");
Thread.Sleep(2000);
Console.WriteLine("Thread has finished.");
}
}
```

In this example, we create a new thread using the Thread class and specify the DoWork method as the entry point. We then start the thread using the Start method. The main thread continues executing other tasks while the new thread is running. We use the Join method to wait for the new thread to complete before continuing with the main thread.

10.2.3 Thread States

A thread can be in one of several states during its lifetime. The ThreadState enumeration in the System.Threading namespace defines the possible states of a thread. Some of the common thread states include:

- Unstarted: The thread has been created but has not yet started.
- Running: The thread is currently executing.
- Stopped: The thread has completed its execution.

- Suspended: The thread has been temporarily paused.
- Aborted: The thread has been forcefully terminated.

You can check the state of a thread using the ThreadState property of the Thread class. For example:

```
Thread thread = new Thread(DoWork);
thread.Start();
// Check the state of the thread
if (thread.ThreadState == ThreadState.Running)
{
Console.WriteLine("Thread is running.");
}
```

10.2.4 Thread Synchronization

When multiple threads access shared resources concurrently, it can lead to synchronization issues and unexpected behavior. To ensure thread safety and prevent race conditions, you can use synchronization techniques such as locks, mutexes, and semaphores.

10.2.4.1 Locks

A lock is a synchronization mechanism that allows only one thread to access a shared resource at a time. In C#, you can use the lock keyword to acquire a lock on an object. This ensures that only one thread can execute the locked code block at a time.

Here's an example of using a lock to synchronize access to a shared resource:

```
using System;
using System.Threading;
public class Program
{
private static object lockObject = new object();
private static int counter = 0;
public static void Main()
```

```
{
Thread thread1 = new Thread(IncrementCounter);
Thread thread2 = new Thread(IncrementCounter);
thread1.Start();
thread2.Start();
thread1.Join();
thread2.Join();
Console.WriteLine("Counter value: " + counter);
}
public static void IncrementCounter()
{
for (int i = 0; i < 100000; i++)
{
lock (lockObject)
{
counter++;
}
}
}
}
```

In this example, we create two threads that increment a shared counter variable. We use the lock keyword to acquire a lock on the lockObject before incrementing the counter. This ensures that only one thread can access the counter at a time, preventing any synchronization issues.

10.2.4.2 Mutexes

A mutex (short for mutual exclusion) is another synchronization mechanism that allows multiple threads to access a shared resource, but only one thread at a time. Unlike locks, mutexes can be used to synchronize access across multiple processes.

In C#, you can use the Mutex class from the System.Threading namespace to create a mutex. Here's an example:

```csharp
using System;
using System.Threading;
public class Program
{
private static Mutex mutex = new Mutex();
private static int counter = 0;
public static void Main()
{
Thread thread1 = new Thread(IncrementCounter);
Thread thread2 = new Thread(IncrementCounter);
thread1.Start();
thread2.Start();
thread1.Join();
thread2.Join();
Console.WriteLine("Counter value: " + counter);
}
public static void IncrementCounter()
{
for (int i = 0; i < 100000; i++)
{
mutex.WaitOne();
counter++;
mutex.ReleaseMutex();
}
}
}
```

In this example, we create two threads that increment a shared counter variable. We use a Mutex object to synchronize access to the counter. The WaitOne method is used to acquire the mutex, and the ReleaseMutex method is used to release it.

10.2.4.3 Semaphores

A semaphore is a synchronization mechanism that allows a specified number of threads to access a shared resource concurrently. It can be used to control access to a resource that has a limited capacity.

In C#, you can use the Semaphore class from the System.Threading namespace to create a semaphore. Here's an example:

```csharp
using System;
using System.Threading;
public class Program
{
private static Semaphore semaphore = new Semaphore(2, 2);
private static int counter = 0;
public static void Main()
{
Thread thread1 = new Thread(IncrementCounter);
Thread thread2 = new Thread(IncrementCounter);
Thread thread3 = new Thread(IncrementCounter);
thread1.Start();
thread2.Start();
thread3.Start();
thread1.Join();
thread2.Join();
thread3.Join();
Console.WriteLine("Counter value: " + counter);
}
public static void IncrementCounter()
{
semaphore.WaitOne();
counter++;
semaphore.Release();
}
```

}

In this example, we create three threads that increment a shared counter variable. We use a Semaphore object with a maximum count of 2 to allow only two threads to access the counter concurrently. The WaitOne method is used to acquire a semaphore slot, and the Release method is used to release it.

10.2.5 Thread Safety

Thread safety is the property of a program that ensures correct behavior when multiple threads access shared resources concurrently. Writing thread-safe code is essential to prevent race conditions, deadlocks, and other synchronization issues.

To write thread-safe code, you should:

- Use synchronization techniques such as locks, mutexes, and semaphores to control access to shared resources.
- Avoid accessing shared resources without proper synchronization.
- Use atomic operations or thread-safe data structures when performing operations on shared resources.

By following these best practices, you can ensure that your code behaves correctly and consistently in a multi-threaded environment.

Conclusion

In this section, we explored how to create and manage threads in C#. We learned how to create a new thread, check its state, and synchronize access to shared resources using locks, mutexes, and semaphores. We also discussed the importance of thread safety and best practices for writing thread-safe code. By mastering the concepts covered in this section, you will be able to leverage the power of multithreading to improve the performance and responsiveness of your C# applications.

10.3 Synchronization and Locking

In multithreaded programming, synchronization and locking are essential concepts to ensure that multiple threads can safely access shared resources without causing data corruption or race conditions. In this section, we will explore various synchronization techniques and locking mechanisms available in C#.

10.3.1 Introduction to Synchronization

Synchronization is the process of coordinating the execution of multiple threads to ensure that they access shared resources in a controlled manner. Without proper synchronization, concurrent access to shared data can lead to unpredictable and erroneous behavior.

In C#, there are several synchronization techniques available, including locks, mutexes, semaphores, and monitors. These techniques provide mechanisms to control access to shared resources and prevent multiple threads from accessing them simultaneously.

10.3.2 Locking with the lock Statement

The lock statement in C# provides a simple and convenient way to synchronize access to shared resources. It ensures that only one thread can execute a specific block of code at a time, preventing other threads from accessing the same code until the lock is released.

The lock statement uses a monitor object to enforce mutual exclusion. When a thread encounters a lock statement, it acquires the lock on the specified monitor object, executes the code within the block, and then releases the lock when it exits the block.

Here's an example that demonstrates the usage of the lock statement:

```
class Counter
{
private int count = 0;
private object lockObject = new object();
public void Increment()
```

```
{
lock (lockObject)
{
count++;
}
}
public int GetCount()
{
lock (lockObject)
{
return count;
}
}
}
```

In the above example, the lockObject is used as a monitor object to synchronize access to the count variable. The Increment and GetCount methods are wrapped inside lock statements, ensuring that only one thread can modify or read the count variable at a time.

10.3.3 Mutexes

A mutex (short for mutual exclusion) is another synchronization primitive available in C#. It provides a more advanced form of locking compared to the lock statement. Unlike the lock statement, which is limited to a single process, a mutex can be used to synchronize access across multiple processes.

A mutex allows only one thread or process to acquire the lock at a time. If a thread or process attempts to acquire the lock while it is already held by another thread or process, it will be blocked until the lock is released.

Here's an example that demonstrates the usage of a mutex:

```
class Counter
{
private int count = 0;
```

```
private Mutex mutex = new Mutex();
public void Increment()
{
mutex.WaitOne();
count++;
mutex.ReleaseMutex();
}
public int GetCount()
{
mutex.WaitOne();
int currentCount = count;
mutex.ReleaseMutex();
return currentCount;
}
}
```

In the above example, the mutex object is used to synchronize access to the count variable. The WaitOne method is called to acquire the lock, and the ReleaseMutex method is called to release the lock.

10.3.4 Semaphores

A semaphore is a synchronization primitive that allows a specified number of threads to access a shared resource concurrently. It maintains a count that represents the number of available resources. When a thread wants to access the resource, it must acquire a semaphore. If the count is greater than zero, the thread can proceed. Otherwise, it will be blocked until a resource becomes available.

In C#, the Semaphore class provides the functionality to work with semaphores. Here's an example that demonstrates the usage of a semaphore:

```
class Printer
{
private Semaphore semaphore = new Semaphore(1, 1);
public void Print(string document)
```

```
{
semaphore.WaitOne();
// Print the document
semaphore.Release();
}
}
```

In the above example, the semaphore object is created with an initial count of 1, indicating that only one thread can access the Print method at a time. The WaitOne method is called to acquire the semaphore, and the Release method is called to release it.

10.3.5 Monitors

Monitors are synchronization primitives that provide a higher-level abstraction for managing access to shared resources. In C#, the Monitor class provides the functionality to work with monitors.

A monitor is similar to a lock but provides additional features such as waiting and signaling. It allows threads to wait for a condition to become true before proceeding. This can be useful in scenarios where a thread needs to wait for a specific condition to be met before continuing its execution.

Here's an example that demonstrates the usage of a monitor:

```
class Printer
{
private object lockObject = new object();
public void Print(string document)
{
lock (lockObject)
{
// Print the document
Monitor.Pulse(lockObject);
}
}
public void WaitForPrint()
```

```
{
lock (lockObject)
{
while (/* condition */)
{
Monitor.Wait(lockObject);
}
}
}
}
```

In the above example, the lockObject is used as a monitor object. The Print method acquires the lock, prints the document, and then signals other threads waiting on the same monitor using the Monitor.Pulse method. The WaitForPrint method waits for a specific condition to be met using the Monitor.Wait method.

Conclusion

Synchronization and locking are crucial aspects of multithreaded programming in C#. They ensure that shared resources are accessed in a controlled and thread-safe manner. In this section, we explored various synchronization techniques, including the lock statement, mutexes, semaphores, and monitors. Understanding and applying these techniques correctly will help you write robust and efficient multithreaded applications in C#.

10.4 Thread Safety

In multi-threaded programming, thread safety refers to the ability of a program or system to function correctly and consistently when multiple threads are executing concurrently. When multiple threads access shared resources or data simultaneously, there is a potential for race conditions and other synchronization issues that can lead to incorrect or unpredictable behavior.

Thread safety is particularly important in C# because it is a language that supports multi-threading and concurrent programming. C# provides various mechanisms and techniques to ensure thread safety and prevent data corruption or inconsistencies when multiple threads are accessing shared resources.

10.4.1 Understanding Thread Safety

Thread safety is achieved by synchronizing access to shared resources or data in a way that ensures only one thread can access the resource at a time. This prevents race conditions where multiple threads try to modify the same data simultaneously, leading to unpredictable results.

There are several common scenarios where thread safety is crucial:

1. **Shared Data**: When multiple threads access and modify the same data concurrently, it is essential to ensure that the data remains consistent and correct.

2. **Mutable Objects**: If an object is mutable (can be modified), and multiple threads access and modify it simultaneously, thread safety measures must be taken to prevent data corruption.

3. **Critical Sections**: Certain sections of code may need to be executed atomically, meaning that only one thread can execute the code at a time. This is often necessary when modifying shared resources or data.

10.4.2 Techniques for Thread Safety

C# provides several techniques and mechanisms to achieve thread safety. Let's explore some of the commonly used ones:

1. **Locking**: The lock keyword in C# is used to create a mutually exclusive lock on a section of code. By enclosing critical sections of code within a lock block, only one thread can execute the code at a time, ensuring thread safety. Locking can be used with any object as a lock, but it is recommended to use a dedicated lock object to prevent unintended locking.

2. **Monitor**: The Monitor class in C# provides synchronization primitives for managing access to shared resources. It allows you to acquire and release locks, wait for signals, and pulse signals to notify waiting threads. The Monitor class is often used in conjunction with the lock keyword to provide more fine-grained control over synchronization.

3. **Thread-Safe Collections**: C# provides thread-safe collection classes such as ConcurrentQueue, ConcurrentStack, and ConcurrentDictionary that are designed to be used in multi-threaded scenarios. These collections internally handle synchronization and ensure thread safety when multiple threads access them concurrently.

4. **Immutable Objects**: Immutable objects are objects whose state cannot be modified after creation. Immutable objects are inherently thread-safe because they cannot be changed once created. By designing classes to be immutable, you can avoid many thread safety issues.

5. **Atomic Operations**: C# provides atomic operations such as Interlocked class methods that perform operations on shared variables atomically. Atomic operations ensure that the operation is completed without interruption from other threads, preventing race conditions.

10.4.3 Best Practices for Thread Safety

To ensure thread safety in your C# programs, consider the following best practices:

1. **Minimize Shared State**: Reduce the amount of shared data between threads as much as possible. Minimizing shared state reduces the chances of race conditions and synchronization issues.

2. **Use Immutable Objects**: Whenever possible, design your classes to be immutable. Immutable objects are inherently thread-safe and eliminate the need for synchronization.

3. **Avoid Global Variables**: Global variables are accessible by all threads and can lead to synchronization issues. Instead, use local variables or pass data explicitly between threads.

4. **Synchronize Access to Shared Resources**: Use locking mechanisms such as the lock keyword or Monitor class to synchronize access to shared resources. Ensure that critical sections of code are properly protected to prevent race conditions.

5. **Use Thread-Safe Collections**: When working with collections that need to be accessed by multiple threads, use thread-safe collection classes such as ConcurrentQueue or ConcurrentDictionary to ensure thread safety.

6. **Avoid Deadlocks**: Deadlocks occur when two or more threads are waiting for each other to release resources, resulting in a deadlock situation. To avoid deadlocks, ensure that locks are acquired and released in the correct order and use timeout mechanisms when waiting for locks.

7. **Test and Debug**: Thoroughly test your multi-threaded code to identify and fix any thread safety issues. Use debugging tools and techniques to analyze and diagnose synchronization problems.

By following these best practices and using the appropriate thread safety techniques, you can ensure that your C# programs function correctly and consistently in multi-threaded environments.

Conclusion

Thread safety is a critical aspect of multi-threaded programming in C#. By understanding the concepts and techniques of thread safety, you can prevent race conditions, synchronization issues, and data corruption in your programs. Use locking mechanisms, thread-safe collections, and immutable objects to synchronize access to shared resources and ensure consistent behavior in multi-threaded scenarios. Remember to follow best practices and thoroughly test your code to identify and fix any thread safety issues.

11 - Advanced Topics

11.1 Delegates and Events

Delegates and events are powerful features in C# that allow you to create flexible and extensible code. They are essential for implementing event-driven programming and are widely used in various applications, including graphical user interfaces, networking, and asynchronous programming.

11.1.1 Understanding Delegates

A delegate is a type that represents a reference to a method. It allows you to treat methods as objects, which can be passed as parameters, stored in variables, and invoked dynamically. Delegates provide a way to decouple the sender of an event from the receiver, enabling loose coupling and separation of concerns.

To define a delegate, you need to specify the signature of the method it can reference. The signature includes the return type and the parameters of the method. Here's an example of a delegate declaration:

delegate void MyDelegate(int x, int y);

In this example, the delegate MyDelegate can reference any method that takes two int parameters and returns void. Once you have defined a delegate, you can create an instance of it and assign it to a method that matches its signature. Here's how you can use the delegate:

```
void Add(int x, int y)
{
int sum = x + y;
Console.WriteLine($"The sum of {x} and {y} is {sum}");
}
MyDelegate myDelegate = Add;
myDelegate(5, 3); // Output: The sum of 5 and 3 is 8
```

In this example, the Add method matches the signature of the MyDelegate delegate, so we can assign it to the delegate instance myDelegate. When we invoke the delegate, it calls the Add method and passes the arguments 5 and 3.

11.1.2 Multicast Delegates

A multicast delegate is a delegate that can hold references to multiple methods. It allows you to combine multiple methods into a single delegate, which can then be invoked to call all the referenced methods in the order they were added. Multicast delegates are useful when you want to raise an event and notify multiple subscribers.

To create a multicast delegate, you can use the += operator to add methods to the delegate's invocation list. Here's an example:

```
delegate void MyMulticastDelegate();
void Method1()
{
Console.WriteLine("Method 1");
}
void Method2()
{
Console.WriteLine("Method 2");
}
MyMulticastDelegate multicastDelegate = Method1;
multicastDelegate += Method2;
multicastDelegate(); // Output: Method 1
// Method 2
```

In this example, we create a multicast delegate MyMulticastDelegate and add two methods Method1 and Method2 to its invocation list. When we invoke the delegate, it calls both methods in the order they were added.

11.1.3 Events

Events are a special type of delegate that provide a standardized way to implement the publisher-subscriber pattern. They allow objects to notify other objects when something of interest happens. Events are widely used in graphical user interfaces to handle user interactions and in asynchronous programming to handle completion or error notifications.

To define an event, you need to declare it using the event keyword and specify the delegate type that will handle the event. Here's an example:

```
class Button
{
public event EventHandler Click;
public void OnClick()
{
Click?.Invoke(this, EventArgs.Empty);
}
}
```

In this example, we define a Button class with an event Click of type EventHandler. The EventHandler delegate is a predefined delegate in C# that represents a method that takes two parameters: the sender of the event and an EventArgs object. The OnClick method is responsible for raising the event by invoking the delegate.

To subscribe to an event, you can use the += operator to add a method to the event's invocation list. Here's an example:

```
Button button = new Button();
button.Click += Button_Click;
void Button_Click(object sender, EventArgs e)
{
Console.WriteLine("Button clicked");
}
```

In this example, we create a Button instance and subscribe to its Click event by adding the Button_Click method to the event's invocation list. When the button is clicked and the event is raised, the Button_Click method is called.

11.1.4 Event Handlers

An event handler is a method that handles an event. It is a method that matches the signature of the delegate associated with the event.

Event handlers are responsible for performing the necessary actions when an event is raised.

When an event is raised, all the event handlers in the invocation list are called sequentially. The order in which the event handlers are called depends on the order in which they were added to the event's invocation list.

Here's an example of an event handler for the Click event of a Button:

```
void Button_Click(object sender, EventArgs e)
{
Console.WriteLine("Button clicked");
}
```

In this example, the event handler takes two parameters: the sender of the event (in this case, the Button object) and an EventArgs object. Inside the event handler, you can perform any actions or logic that need to be executed when the event is raised.

11.1.5 Event Accessors

Events in C# have two accessors: add and remove. These accessors allow you to control the subscription and unsubscription of event handlers. By default, events are implemented with an implicit add accessor and an implicit remove accessor.

Here's an example of how to explicitly define the add and remove accessors for an event:

```
class Button
{
private EventHandler _click;
public event EventHandler Click
{
add { _click += value; }
remove { _click -= value; }
}
public void OnClick()
```

```
{
    _click?.Invoke(this, EventArgs.Empty);
}
}
```

In this example, we define a private field _click of type EventHandler to store the event handlers. The add accessor adds a new event handler to the invocation list, and the remove accessor removes an event handler from the invocation list.

By explicitly defining the add and remove accessors, you have more control over the subscription and unsubscription process. You can perform additional logic or validation before adding or removing an event handler.

11.1.6 Summary

Delegates and events are powerful features in C# that enable you to create flexible and extensible code. Delegates allow you to treat methods as objects and provide a way to decouple the sender of an event from the receiver. Events provide a standardized way to implement the publisher-subscriber pattern and allow objects to notify other objects when something of interest happens.

In this section, you learned about delegates, multicast delegates, events, event handlers, and event accessors. Understanding these concepts is crucial for mastering C# and building robust and scalable applications.

11.2 Generics

Generics are a powerful feature in C# that allow you to create reusable code by writing classes, methods, and structures that can work with different data types. With generics, you can create classes and methods that are type-safe and can be used with any data type, providing flexibility and efficiency in your code.

11.2.1 Introduction to Generics

Generics were introduced in C# 2.0 and have since become an essential part of the language. They provide a way to write code that is not specific to any particular data type, but can be used with multiple types. This allows you to write more flexible and reusable code, reducing the need for duplication and improving the overall design of your application.

The main benefit of using generics is that they provide type safety. By using generics, you can ensure that the code you write will work correctly with any data type, without the need for explicit type casting or conversion. This helps catch errors at compile-time rather than at runtime, making your code more reliable and easier to maintain.

11.2.2 Creating Generic Classes

In C#, you can create generic classes by using the class keyword followed by the name of the class and the type parameter in angle brackets. The type parameter represents a placeholder for the actual data type that will be used when an instance of the class is created.

Here's an example of a generic class that represents a stack data structure:

```
public class Stack<T>
{
private List<T> items;
public Stack()
{
items = new List<T>();
```

```
}
public void Push(T item)
{
items.Add(item);
}
public T Pop()
{
if (items.Count == 0)
{
throw new InvalidOperationException("Stack is empty");
}
T item = items[items.Count - 1];
items.RemoveAt(items.Count - 1);
return item;
}
}
```

In this example, the Stack<T> class is defined with a type parameter T. This allows the class to work with any data type. The Push method adds an item of type T to the stack, while the Pop method removes and returns the top item from the stack.

11.2.3 Using Generic Classes

To use a generic class, you need to specify the actual data type that will be used when creating an instance of the class. This is done by providing the type argument in angle brackets after the class name.

Here's an example of how to use the Stack<T> class:

```
Stack<int> intStack = new Stack<int>();
intStack.Push(10);
intStack.Push(20);
intStack.Push(30);
int item = intStack.Pop(); // item = 30
```

In this example, an instance of the Stack<int> class is created, which means the stack will work with integers. The Push method is used to add three integers to the stack, and the Pop method is used to retrieve the top item from the stack.

11.2.4 Generic Methods

In addition to generic classes, C# also supports generic methods. Generic methods allow you to write methods that can work with different data types, similar to generic classes.

Here's an example of a generic method that swaps two values:

```
public static void Swap<T>(ref T a, ref T b)
{
T temp = a;
a = b;
b = temp;
}
```

In this example, the Swap method is defined with a type parameter T. This allows the method to work with any data type. The method takes two parameters of type T by reference and swaps their values.

To use the Swap method, you can provide the type argument explicitly or let the compiler infer the type argument based on the types of the arguments:

```
int a = 10;
int b = 20;
Swap<int>(ref a, ref b); // a = 20, b = 10
string x = "hello";
string y = "world";
Swap(ref x, ref y); // x = "world", y = "hello"
```

In this example, the Swap method is called twice, once with integers and once with strings. The type argument is provided explicitly for the first call, while the compiler infers the type argument for the second call based on the types of the arguments.

11.2.5 Constraints on Type Parameters

In some cases, you may want to restrict the types that can be used as type arguments in a generic class or method. This can be done by using type parameter constraints.

Type parameter constraints allow you to specify that a type parameter must be a specific type or must implement certain interfaces. This helps ensure that the code you write will work correctly with the specified types.

Here's an example of a generic class with a type parameter constraint:

```
public class Calculator<T> where T : struct, IComparable<T>
{
public T Add(T a, T b)
{
return (dynamic)a + (dynamic)b;
}
}
```

In this example, the Calculator<T> class is defined with a type parameter T that must be a value type (struct) and must implement the IComparable<T> interface. This constraint ensures that the Add method can be used with numeric types that can be compared.

```
Calculator<int> intCalculator = new Calculator<int>();
int sum = intCalculator.Add(10, 20); // sum = 30
Calculator<string> stringCalculator = new Calculator<string>();
// Compile-time error
```

In this example, an instance of the Calculator<int> class is created, which means the Add method can be used with integers. However, when trying to create an instance of the Calculator<string> class, a compile-time error occurs because strings do not satisfy the type parameter constraint.

11.2.6 Benefits of Using Generics

Using generics in your code offers several benefits:

- Reusability: Generics allow you to write code that can be used with different data types, reducing the need for duplication and improving code reuse.

- Type safety: Generics provide type safety by catching errors at compile-time rather than at runtime. This helps prevent type-related bugs and makes your code more reliable.
- Performance: Generics can improve performance by avoiding the need for boxing and unboxing operations, which can be expensive in terms of memory and CPU usage.
- Code readability: Generics make your code more readable and maintainable by providing a clear and concise way to work with different data types.

By understanding and utilizing generics effectively, you can write more flexible and efficient code in C#. Generics are a powerful feature that can greatly enhance the design and functionality of your applications.

11.3 LINQ

LINQ (Language Integrated Query) is a powerful feature in C# that allows you to query and manipulate data from different data sources using a unified syntax. It provides a convenient way to work with collections, databases, XML, and other data sources in a consistent and efficient manner. LINQ combines the power of SQL-like queries with the flexibility and expressiveness of C#.

11.3.1 Introduction to LINQ

LINQ was introduced in C# 3.0 as a language feature that enables developers to write queries directly in their code. It provides a set of standard query operators that can be used to perform various operations on data, such as filtering, sorting, grouping, and projecting. LINQ queries are written using a declarative syntax, which makes them easy to read and understand.

The main advantage of using LINQ is that it allows you to write concise and expressive code. Instead of writing complex loops and conditional statements, you can use LINQ to express your intentions in a more natural and intuitive way. LINQ also promotes code reuse and modularity, as queries can be easily composed and reused across different parts of your application.

11.3.2 LINQ Query Syntax

LINQ provides two syntax options for writing queries: query syntax and method syntax. Query syntax is similar to SQL and allows you to write queries in a more declarative and intuitive way. Method syntax, on the other hand, uses method calls to chain together query operators and is more concise and flexible.

Here's an example of a LINQ query written in query syntax:

```
var result = from student in students
where student.Age > 18
orderby student.Name
select student;
```

In this example, we are querying a collection of students and selecting those who are older than 18, ordering them by their names. The result is a new collection that contains the selected students.

The same query can be written using method syntax as follows:

```
var result = students
.Where(student => student.Age > 18)
.OrderBy(student => student.Name)
.Select(student => student);
```

Both query syntax and method syntax are equivalent and produce the same result. The choice between them is mostly a matter of personal preference and readability.

11.3.3 LINQ Operators

LINQ provides a rich set of operators that can be used to perform various operations on data. These operators can be categorized into three main types: filtering operators, projection operators, and aggregation operators.

Filtering operators allow you to filter data based on a specified condition. Some commonly used filtering operators include Where, OfType, and Take.

Projection operators allow you to transform data into a different shape or format. Some commonly used projection operators include Select, SelectMany, and GroupBy.

Aggregation operators allow you to perform calculations on data, such as counting, summing, averaging, and finding the maximum or minimum value. Some commonly used aggregation operators include Count, Sum, Average, Max, and Min.

LINQ also provides operators for joining multiple data sources, sorting data, and performing set operations such as union, intersection, and difference.

11.3.4 LINQ to Objects

LINQ can be used to query and manipulate data from various data sources. One of the most common use cases is querying in-memory collections, also known as LINQ to Objects. LINQ to Objects allows you to query and manipulate data stored in arrays, lists, dictionaries, and other collection types.

Here's an example of using LINQ to Objects to filter and project data from a list of students:

```
var result = from student in students
where student.Age > 18
orderby student.Name
select new { student.Name, student.Age };
```

In this example, we are selecting the names and ages of students who are older than 18 and ordering them by their names. The result is a new collection of anonymous objects that contain the selected properties.

LINQ to Objects provides a convenient and efficient way to work with in-memory data. It allows you to write expressive and readable code for querying and manipulating collections.

11.3.5 LINQ to SQL

LINQ to SQL is a component of LINQ that allows you to query and manipulate data from relational databases using LINQ syntax. It provides a mapping between database tables and C# classes, allowing you to query and update data using LINQ queries.

To use LINQ to SQL, you need to create a data context class that represents the database and its tables. The data context class provides properties for accessing the tables and methods for executing queries and updates.

Here's an example of using LINQ to SQL to query data from a database:

```
using (var context = new DataContext())
{
var result = from customer in context.Customers
where customer.City == "New York"
select customer;
```

}

In this example, we are querying the customers table and selecting those who are located in New York. The result is a collection of customer objects.

LINQ to SQL provides a convenient and type-safe way to work with relational databases. It allows you to write queries using LINQ syntax and benefit from compile-time checking and IntelliSense.

11.3.6 LINQ to XML

LINQ to XML is a component of LINQ that allows you to query and manipulate XML data using LINQ syntax. It provides a set of query operators that can be used to traverse and manipulate XML documents.

To use LINQ to XML, you need to load an XML document into an XDocument object. The XDocument object represents the XML document and provides methods for querying and manipulating its contents.

Here's an example of using LINQ to XML to query data from an XML document:

```
var document = XDocument.Load("data.xml");
var result = from element in document.Descendants("book")
where (string)element.Element("author") == "John Doe"
select element;
```

In this example, we are querying an XML document and selecting the book elements whose author is "John Doe". The result is a collection of XElement objects representing the selected elements.

LINQ to XML provides a powerful and expressive way to work with XML data. It allows you to query and manipulate XML documents using a familiar and intuitive syntax.

11.3.7 LINQ Performance Considerations

When using LINQ, it's important to consider performance implications, especially when working with large data sets. LINQ queries are executed lazily, which means that the query is not executed until the result is actually enumerated.

To improve performance, you can use techniques such as filtering data early in the query, using appropriate data structures, and optimizing database queries. You can also use caching and memoization techniques to avoid executing the same query multiple times.

It's also important to be aware of the limitations of LINQ and choose the appropriate tool for the job. While LINQ provides a convenient and expressive way to work with data, there are cases where using raw SQL or other specialized tools may be more efficient.

Conclusion

LINQ is a powerful feature in C# that allows you to query and manipulate data from different data sources using a unified syntax. It provides a convenient and expressive way to work with collections, databases, XML, and other data sources. By mastering LINQ, you can write more concise and readable code and improve the efficiency and maintainability of your applications.

11.4 Attributes

Attributes are a powerful feature in C# that allow you to add metadata to your code. They provide a way to attach additional information to various program elements such as classes, methods, properties, and parameters. This metadata can be used by the compiler, runtime, or other tools to perform specific actions or make decisions based on the information provided by the attributes.

11.4.1 Introduction to Attributes

Attributes are defined using square brackets ([]) placed before the target element they are applied to. They consist of a name followed by an optional list of parameters enclosed in parentheses. The parameters can be positional or named, and they provide additional information to the attribute.

For example, consider the following attribute declaration:

```
[Serializable]
public class MyClass
{
// class implementation
}
```

In this example, the Serializable attribute is applied to the MyClass class. This attribute indicates that instances of the class can be serialized, which means they can be converted into a format that can be stored or transmitted and then reconstructed back into an object.

11.4.2 Predefined Attributes

C# provides a set of predefined attributes that can be used to add specific behavior or information to your code. These attributes are defined in the System namespace and can be applied to various program elements.

Some commonly used predefined attributes include:

- Obsolete: Marks a program element as obsolete or deprecated, indicating that it should no longer be used.

- DllImport: Specifies that a method is implemented in an external DLL (Dynamic-Link Library).
- Conditional: Specifies that a method should be called only if a specified compilation symbol is defined.
- Serializable: Indicates that a class can be serialized.
- AttributeUsage: Specifies how an attribute class can be used.

These predefined attributes can be applied to classes, methods, properties, parameters, and other program elements to provide additional information or behavior.

11.4.3 Creating Custom Attributes

In addition to using predefined attributes, you can also create your own custom attributes in C#. Custom attributes allow you to define your own metadata and attach it to your code elements.

To create a custom attribute, you need to define a new class and apply the AttributeUsage attribute to it. This attribute specifies how the custom attribute can be used and provides additional information about its usage.

Here's an example of a custom attribute:

```
[AttributeUsage(AttributeTargets.Class)]
public class MyCustomAttribute : Attribute
{
public string Description { get; set; }
public MyCustomAttribute(string description)
{
Description = description;
}
}
```

In this example, we define a custom attribute called MyCustomAttribute. It inherits from the Attribute base class and has a single property called Description. The attribute can be applied only to classes (AttributeTargets.Class).

To use this custom attribute, you can apply it to a class as follows:

```
[MyCustom("This is a custom attribute")]
public class MyClass
{
// class implementation
}
```

In this case, the MyCustom attribute is applied to the MyClass class with the specified description. You can then retrieve this information at runtime using reflection.

11.4.4 Reflection and Attributes

Reflection is a powerful feature in C# that allows you to inspect and manipulate code at runtime. It provides a way to examine the metadata of types, methods, properties, and other program elements.

Attributes play a crucial role in reflection as they provide additional metadata that can be accessed and analyzed at runtime. Using reflection, you can retrieve the attributes applied to a specific program element and perform actions based on the information provided by those attributes.

For example, you can use reflection to retrieve the custom attribute applied to a class and extract its properties:

```
Type type = typeof(MyClass);
MyCustomAttribute                    attribute                    =
(MyCustomAttribute)type.GetCustomAttribute(typeof(MyCustomA
if (attribute != null)
{
Console.WriteLine(attribute.Description);
}
```

In this example, we use reflection to retrieve the MyCustomAttribute applied to the MyClass class. We then cast it to the appropriate type and access its Description property.

Reflection and attributes provide a powerful combination that allows you to add dynamic behavior to your code based on the metadata provided by the attributes.

11.4.5 Attribute Targets

Attributes can be applied to various program elements, known as attribute targets. Some common attribute targets include:

- Classes
- Methods
- Properties
- Fields
- Parameters
- Events
- Delegates
- Enums
- Interfaces

Each attribute has specific rules regarding which targets it can be applied to. For example, the Serializable attribute can only be applied to classes, while the Obsolete attribute can be applied to methods, properties, and other program elements.

Understanding the available attribute targets is important when creating or using attributes in your code.

11.4.6 Attribute Usage Guidelines

When using attributes, it's important to follow certain guidelines to ensure their proper usage and effectiveness. Here are some general guidelines to keep in mind:

- Use attributes sparingly: Only apply attributes when necessary and avoid overusing them. Too many attributes can clutter your code and make it harder to read and maintain.
- Use predefined attributes whenever possible: Predefined attributes provide well-defined behavior and are widely

recognized by tools and frameworks. If a predefined attribute meets your requirements, use it instead of creating a custom attribute.

- Document your custom attributes: When creating custom attributes, provide clear documentation on their purpose, usage, and any specific guidelines or restrictions.
- Consider attribute inheritance: By default, attributes are not inherited by derived classes. If you want an attribute to be inherited, you need to specify the Inherited property of the AttributeUsage attribute.
- Be aware of attribute order: The order in which attributes are applied can sometimes affect their behavior. Make sure to understand the order of attribute evaluation and any potential interactions between attributes.

By following these guidelines, you can effectively use attributes to enhance your code and provide additional metadata that can be used by the compiler, runtime, or other tools.

Conclusion

Attributes are a powerful feature in C# that allow you to add metadata to your code. They provide a way to attach additional information to various program elements, which can be used by the compiler, runtime, or other tools. In this section, you learned about the basics of attributes, including predefined attributes, creating custom attributes, using reflection with attributes, attribute targets, and attribute usage guidelines. By understanding and effectively using attributes, you can enhance the functionality and behavior of your C# programs.

12 - Debugging and Testing

12.1 Debugging Techniques

Debugging is an essential skill for any programmer. It involves identifying and fixing errors or bugs in your code to ensure that it runs smoothly and produces the desired results. In this section, we will explore various debugging techniques that can help you effectively troubleshoot and resolve issues in your C# programs.

12.1.1 Understanding the Debugging Process

Before diving into specific debugging techniques, it is important to understand the overall process of debugging. The debugging process typically involves the following steps:

1. **Reproduce the Issue**: The first step in debugging is to reproduce the issue or error that you are encountering. This involves identifying the specific scenario or input that triggers the problem.

2. **Identify the Cause**: Once you have reproduced the issue, the next step is to identify the root cause of the problem. This can be done by analyzing the code and understanding how it is supposed to work.

3. **Isolate the Problem**: After identifying the cause, it is important to isolate the problem. This involves narrowing down the code or specific section that is causing the issue.

4. **Use Debugging Tools**: C# provides a range of debugging tools that can help you analyze and understand the behavior of your code. These tools include breakpoints, watch windows, and step-by-step execution.

5. **Analyze Variables and Data**: While debugging, it is crucial to analyze the values of variables and data at different points in the code. This can help you identify any unexpected or incorrect values that may be causing the issue.

6. **Fix the Issue**: Once you have identified the cause and isolated

the problem, the final step is to fix the issue. This may involve making changes to the code, updating variables, or modifying the logic to ensure that the program functions correctly.

12.1.2 Using Breakpoints

One of the most commonly used debugging techniques is the use of breakpoints. A breakpoint is a marker that you can set in your code to pause the execution at a specific line. This allows you to analyze the state of the program and the values of variables at that point.

To set a breakpoint in Visual Studio, simply click on the left margin of the code editor next to the line where you want to pause the execution. When the program reaches that line during execution, it will pause, and you can analyze the variables and data.

While the program is paused at a breakpoint, you can use the debugging tools provided by Visual Studio to step through the code, view variable values, and analyze the program's behavior. This can help you identify any issues or unexpected behavior in your code.

12.1.3 Using Watch Windows

Watch windows are another useful debugging tool that allows you to monitor the values of variables and expressions as your program executes. You can add variables or expressions to the watch window, and their values will be displayed in real-time as the program runs.

To add a variable or expression to the watch window, simply right-click on the variable or expression in the code editor and select "Add Watch". The value of the variable or expression will then be displayed in the watch window.

Using watch windows can be particularly helpful when you want to track the value of a specific variable or expression throughout the execution of your program. This can help you identify any unexpected changes or incorrect values that may be causing issues.

12.1.4 Stepping Through Code

Stepping through code is another powerful debugging technique that allows you to execute your program line by line, analyzing the behavior and values at each step. This can help you understand how the program is executing and identify any issues or unexpected behavior.

Visual Studio provides several options for stepping through code, including:

- **Step Over**: This option allows you to execute the current line of code and move to the next line. If the current line contains a method call, the method will be executed, but the execution will not break inside the method.
- **Step Into**: This option allows you to step into a method call and continue debugging inside the method. This can be useful when you want to analyze the behavior of a specific method or understand how it is being executed.
- **Step Out**: This option allows you to step out of the current method and continue debugging at the calling method. This can be useful when you want to quickly move out of a method and analyze the behavior of the calling code.

By using these stepping options, you can carefully analyze the execution of your program and identify any issues or unexpected behavior.

12.1.5 Analyzing Exception Details

Exceptions are a common type of error that can occur in your code. When an exception is thrown, it can disrupt the normal flow of execution and cause your program to crash or produce incorrect results.

When an exception occurs, it is important to analyze the exception details to understand the cause of the error. Visual Studio provides a detailed exception window that displays information about the exception, including the type of exception, the stack trace, and any inner exceptions.

By analyzing the exception details, you can gain insights into the cause of the error and take appropriate steps to fix it. This may involve modifying the code, handling the exception, or adding error handling mechanisms to prevent similar issues in the future.

12.1.6 Using Debugging Tools

In addition to breakpoints, watch windows, and stepping through code, Visual Studio provides several other debugging tools that can help you analyze and understand the behavior of your code.

Some of these tools include:

- **Immediate Window**: The immediate window allows you to execute code and evaluate expressions during debugging. This can be useful when you want to test a specific expression or execute a line of code to understand its behavior.
- **Call Stack**: The call stack window displays the sequence of method calls that led to the current point of execution. This can help you understand the flow of execution and identify any issues or unexpected behavior.
- **Memory Windows**: Memory windows allow you to analyze the memory usage of your program. You can view the values stored in memory locations, analyze memory addresses, and track memory changes during execution.

By utilizing these debugging tools effectively, you can gain a deeper understanding of your code's behavior and identify and fix any issues or bugs that may be present.

Conclusion

Debugging is an essential skill for any programmer. By understanding the debugging process and utilizing various debugging techniques and tools, you can effectively identify and fix issues in your C# programs. Whether it's setting breakpoints, using watch windows, stepping through code, analyzing exception details, or utilizing other debugging tools, the goal is to gain insights into the behavior of your code and resolve any issues that may arise. With practice and experience, you can become proficient in debugging and ensure that your C# programs run smoothly and produce the desired results.

12.2 Unit Testing

Unit testing is an essential part of software development that helps ensure the quality and reliability of your code. It involves writing test cases to verify the behavior of individual units or components of your code. In this section, we will explore the concept of unit testing and learn how to write effective unit tests using various testing frameworks available for C#.

12.2.1 Introduction to Unit Testing

Unit testing is a software testing technique where individual units or components of a software system are tested independently. The purpose of unit testing is to validate that each unit of the software performs as expected. A unit can be a method, a class, or even a small piece of code.

Unit tests are typically written by developers themselves and are executed frequently during the development process. They help identify bugs and issues early on, making it easier to fix them before they become more complex and costly to resolve.

12.2.2 Benefits of Unit Testing

Unit testing offers several benefits that contribute to the overall quality and maintainability of your code:

1. **Early Bug Detection**: By writing unit tests, you can identify bugs and issues in your code early in the development process. This allows you to fix them before they propagate to other parts of the system, making debugging easier and reducing the overall cost of fixing defects.

2. **Improved Code Quality**: Unit tests act as a safety net for your code. They ensure that each unit of your code behaves as expected and meets the specified requirements. This leads to higher code quality and reduces the chances of introducing regressions when making changes to the codebase.

3. **Code Documentation**: Unit tests serve as a form of documentation for your code. They provide examples of how to use each unit and what results to expect. This makes it easier for other developers to understand and work with your code.

4. **Refactoring Support**: Unit tests provide confidence when refactoring or making changes to your code. They act as a safety net, ensuring that the behavior of the code remains unchanged after modifications. If a unit test fails after a change, it indicates that the modification has introduced a regression.

5. **Faster Development**: Although writing unit tests may initially require additional effort, they can actually speed up the development process in the long run. By catching bugs early and providing a safety net for refactoring, unit tests reduce the time spent on debugging and ensure that the codebase remains stable.

12.2.3 Writing Unit Tests

To write effective unit tests, you need to follow some best practices and guidelines. Here are some key steps to consider when writing unit tests:

1. **Identify Test Scenarios**: Before writing unit tests, identify the different scenarios and use cases that need to be tested. Each test scenario should focus on a specific behavior or functionality of the unit being tested.

2. **Arrange, Act, and Assert**: The structure of a unit test typically follows the "Arrange, Act, and Assert" pattern. In the Arrange phase, you set up the necessary preconditions for the test. In the Act phase, you execute the unit being tested. Finally, in the Assert phase, you verify the expected behavior or outcome of the unit.

3. **Use Test Frameworks**: C# provides several testing

frameworks that simplify the process of writing and executing unit tests. Some popular frameworks include NUnit, xUnit, and MSTest. These frameworks provide a rich set of features for organizing and running tests, as well as assertions for verifying expected results.

4. **Isolate Dependencies**: When writing unit tests, it's important to isolate the unit being tested from its dependencies. This can be achieved by using techniques such as mocking or stubbing. By isolating dependencies, you can focus on testing the behavior of the unit itself without worrying about the correctness of its dependencies.

5. **Test Coverage**: Aim for high test coverage, which means ensuring that your tests cover as much of the codebase as possible. This helps identify areas of the code that are not adequately tested and reduces the risk of undiscovered bugs.

6. **Test Naming and Organization**: Use descriptive and meaningful names for your tests to make them more readable and maintainable. Organize your tests into logical groups or categories to improve test discoverability and maintainability.

12.2.4 Test-Driven Development (TDD)

Test-Driven Development (TDD) is a software development approach that emphasizes writing tests before writing the actual code. With TDD, you start by writing a failing test case that describes the desired behavior of the code. Then, you write the minimum amount of code necessary to make the test pass. Finally, you refactor the code to improve its design and maintainability.

TDD promotes a test-first mindset, where tests drive the development process. It helps ensure that the code is testable, modular, and follows the Single Responsibility Principle (SRP). TDD also encourages developers to think about the design and behavior of the code upfront, leading to cleaner and more maintainable code.

12.2.5 Continuous Integration and Unit Testing

Unit testing plays a crucial role in the context of continuous integration (CI). CI is a development practice where developers frequently integrate their code changes into a shared repository. Each integration triggers an automated build and test process to detect integration issues early.

By including unit tests in the CI pipeline, you can ensure that the codebase remains stable and functional after each integration. This helps catch integration issues and regressions early, allowing for faster feedback and reducing the risk of breaking the build.

Conclusion

Unit testing is an essential practice for ensuring the quality and reliability of your code. By writing effective unit tests, you can catch bugs early, improve code quality, and facilitate refactoring. Test-driven development (TDD) and continuous integration (CI) further enhance the benefits of unit testing by promoting a test-first mindset and ensuring code stability throughout the development process.

12.3 Code Analysis

Code analysis is an essential part of the software development process. It involves examining the source code of a program to identify potential issues, improve code quality, and ensure adherence to coding standards. In this section, we will explore the concept of code analysis and how it can benefit developers in writing robust and maintainable C# code.

12.3.1 What is Code Analysis?

Code analysis, also known as static code analysis, is the process of automatically examining source code to detect potential bugs, security vulnerabilities, and other code quality issues. It is performed without executing the code and can be done using specialized tools or integrated development environments (IDEs) that support code analysis.

The primary goal of code analysis is to identify and fix issues early in the development cycle, reducing the likelihood of bugs and improving the overall quality of the software. By analyzing the code, developers can catch common programming mistakes, enforce coding standards, and ensure compliance with best practices.

12.3.2 Benefits of Code Analysis

Code analysis offers several benefits to developers and development teams. Let's explore some of the key advantages:

1. Bug Detection:

Code analysis tools can identify potential bugs and programming errors, such as null reference exceptions, resource leaks, and incorrect use of APIs. By catching these issues early, developers can prevent bugs from reaching production and improve the stability of their applications.

2. Code Quality Improvement:

Code analysis helps enforce coding standards and best practices, ensuring consistent and maintainable code. It can detect issues like unused variables, unreachable code, and inefficient algorithms, allowing developers to make necessary improvements and optimize their code.

3. Security Vulnerability Detection:

Code analysis tools can identify security vulnerabilities, such as SQL injection, cross-site scripting (XSS), and insecure cryptographic algorithms. By detecting these vulnerabilities early, developers can implement appropriate security measures and protect their applications from potential attacks.

4. Performance Optimization:

Code analysis can highlight performance bottlenecks and inefficient code patterns. By identifying areas of code that consume excessive resources or execute slowly, developers can optimize their code and improve the overall performance of their applications.

5. Maintainability and Readability:

Code analysis tools can enforce coding conventions and guidelines, making the code more readable and maintainable. By ensuring consistent naming conventions, proper code documentation, and adherence to coding standards, developers can enhance the understandability and maintainability of their codebase.

12.3.3 Code Analysis Tools

There are several code analysis tools available for C# that can help developers analyze their code and identify potential issues. Let's explore some popular tools:

1. Visual Studio's Code Analysis:

Visual Studio, the popular IDE for C# development, provides built-in code analysis features. It offers a wide range of rules that can be enabled to analyze the code for potential issues. Visual Studio's code analysis can be run manually or integrated into the build process to ensure continuous analysis.

2. ReSharper:

ReSharper is a popular productivity tool for C# developers that includes powerful code analysis capabilities. It provides real-time code inspections, suggestions, and quick-fixes to improve code quality. ReSharper can be integrated with Visual Studio and offers a comprehensive set of code analysis rules.

3. SonarQube:

SonarQube is an open-source platform for continuous code quality inspection. It supports multiple programming languages, including C#. SonarQube provides a wide range of code analysis rules and metrics to measure code quality. It can be integrated into the build process to ensure continuous code analysis.

4. StyleCop:

StyleCop is a static code analysis tool specifically designed for C#. It enforces a set of coding conventions and guidelines to ensure consistent code style and readability. StyleCop can be integrated with Visual Studio and provides real-time code analysis and suggestions.

12.3.4 Using Code Analysis in C#

To use code analysis in C#, developers can leverage the built-in features of their IDE or use third-party tools. Let's explore how code analysis can be integrated into the development process:

1. Enabling Code Analysis Rules:

Developers can enable specific code analysis rules based on their requirements. These rules can be customized to enforce coding standards, best practices, and specific project requirements. By enabling the appropriate rules, developers can ensure that their code adheres to the desired quality standards.

2. Running Code Analysis:

Code analysis can be run manually or integrated into the build process. Running code analysis manually allows developers to analyze specific code files or projects on-demand. Integrating code analysis into the build process ensures that the code is analyzed automatically during each build, providing continuous feedback on code quality.

3. Fixing Code Analysis Issues:

Code analysis tools provide suggestions and quick-fixes to resolve identified issues. Developers can use these suggestions to fix potential bugs, improve code quality, and ensure compliance with coding standards. By addressing code analysis issues promptly, developers can maintain a high level of code quality throughout the development process.

12.3.5 Conclusion

Code analysis is a valuable practice for developers working with C#. By leveraging code analysis tools and integrating them into the development process, developers can identify potential issues, improve code quality, and ensure adherence to coding standards. Code analysis helps catch bugs early, enforce best practices, and optimize code performance, leading to more robust and maintainable software. Incorporating code analysis into the development workflow can significantly enhance the overall quality of C# applications.

12.4 Performance Testing

Performance testing is a crucial aspect of software development that focuses on evaluating the speed, responsiveness, stability, and scalability of an application under various conditions. It helps identify bottlenecks, optimize code, and ensure that the application meets the performance requirements set by the stakeholders. In this section, we will explore the importance of performance testing, different types of performance tests, and some best practices to follow.

12.4.1 Importance of Performance Testing

Performance testing plays a vital role in ensuring that an application can handle the expected workload efficiently. It helps identify performance issues early in the development cycle, allowing developers to address them before the application is deployed to production. Here are some key reasons why performance testing is important:

1. **User Experience:** Performance testing helps ensure that the application provides a smooth and responsive user experience. It helps identify and fix any performance-related issues that may impact user satisfaction.

2. **Scalability:** Performance testing helps determine how well the application can handle an increasing number of users, transactions, or data volumes. It helps identify scalability bottlenecks and allows developers to optimize the application's performance.

3. **Reliability:** Performance testing helps uncover any stability or reliability issues in the application. It helps identify memory leaks, resource contention, or other issues that may cause the application to crash or become unresponsive.

4. **Optimization:** Performance testing provides valuable insights into the performance characteristics of the

application. It helps identify areas of the code that can be optimized to improve overall performance.

5. **Capacity Planning:** Performance testing helps determine the hardware and infrastructure requirements for the application. It helps estimate the resources needed to support the expected workload and ensures that the infrastructure can handle the anticipated user load.

12.4.2 Types of Performance Tests

There are several types of performance tests that can be conducted to evaluate different aspects of an application's performance. Let's explore some of the commonly used performance tests:

1. **Load Testing:** Load testing involves simulating a realistic workload on the application to measure its performance under normal and peak load conditions. It helps identify performance bottlenecks, such as slow response times or high resource utilization.

2. **Stress Testing:** Stress testing involves pushing the application beyond its normal operating limits to evaluate its behavior under extreme conditions. It helps identify the breaking point of the application and assess its ability to recover gracefully.

3. **Endurance Testing:** Endurance testing involves running the application under a sustained workload for an extended period to evaluate its performance and stability over time. It helps identify any memory leaks, resource leaks, or performance degradation that may occur over long durations.

4. **Scalability Testing:** Scalability testing involves measuring the application's performance as the workload is increased by adding more users, transactions, or data volumes. It helps identify any scalability bottlenecks and assess the application's ability to handle increased load.

5. **Concurrency Testing:** Concurrency testing involves

evaluating the application's performance when multiple users or processes access the system simultaneously. It helps identify any synchronization issues, deadlocks, or resource contention that may occur under concurrent access.

12.4.3 Best Practices for Performance Testing

To ensure effective performance testing, it is essential to follow some best practices. Here are some guidelines to consider:

1. **Define Performance Goals:** Clearly define the performance goals and requirements for the application. This includes response time, throughput, resource utilization, and scalability targets.

2. **Test Early and Often:** Start performance testing early in the development cycle and continue testing at regular intervals. This allows for early identification and resolution of performance issues.

3. **Use Realistic Test Data:** Use realistic test data that closely resembles the production environment. This includes data volumes, user profiles, and transaction patterns.

4. **Monitor System Resources:** Monitor system resources such as CPU, memory, disk I/O, and network utilization during performance tests. This helps identify any resource bottlenecks that may impact performance.

5. **Isolate Performance Tests:** Perform performance tests in isolated environments to minimize interference from other applications or processes. This ensures accurate measurement of the application's performance.

6. **Automate Performance Tests:** Automate performance tests to ensure consistency and repeatability. This allows for easy regression testing and comparison of performance metrics across different test runs.

7. **Analyze and Optimize:** Analyze the performance test results

to identify performance bottlenecks. Optimize the code, database queries, or infrastructure configuration to improve performance.

8. **Test with Production-like Load:** Test the application with a load that closely resembles the expected production workload. This helps ensure that the application can handle the anticipated user load.

9. **Monitor and Tune Production Environment:** Continuously monitor the production environment and tune the application based on real-world performance data. This helps ensure optimal performance in the live environment.

By following these best practices, developers can effectively identify and address performance issues, resulting in a high-performing and reliable application.

Conclusion

Performance testing is a critical aspect of software development that helps ensure the application meets the performance requirements set by the stakeholders. It helps identify performance bottlenecks, optimize code, and ensure a smooth and responsive user experience. By conducting various types of performance tests and following best practices, developers can build high-performing applications that can handle the expected workload efficiently.